MW01644192

Setting Myself On Fire

How I Doused The Flames Of Meth Addiction

TRAVIS MORSE

Edited by Danielle Swanson

DISCLAIMER

This book is not intended to encourage, endorse, glamorize, or in any way make light of unlawful or immoral activities, especially illegal drug use. Drug addiction is a serious disease requiring the help of professionals to treat it. If you are abusing drugs or other substances, please take advantage of the local services, programs, facilities, and organizations available to help you quit.

In this memoir, the author has tried to recreate events, locales, conversations, and experiences from his recollection. In some instances, events and dialog has been compressed to convey the substance of what was said or occurred. To protect privacy, in some instances names of individuals, places, identifying characteristics, physical properties, occupations, and places of residence that are not critically important to understanding the message have been changed.

The following names, listed in alphabetical order, are pseudonyms: Agnes, Becky, Billy, Brad, Damon, Donnie, Ethan, Joshua, Lucas, Marcie, Mark, Martell, Nick, Nikki, Phil, Ray, Sean, and Valerie. The following places are fictitious: Murphy's Tavern, Bad Dog Bar & Grill, and Outlook Tavern.

ISBN: 9798849336534

DEDICATION

To all those who supported me throughout my life regardless of my sins including mom, step-dad Chris, brother Tyler, son Tanner, and my grandmother Nanny.

TABLE OF CONTENTS

ACKNOWLEDGMENTS

First and foremost, thank you Lord Jesus Christ for planting a seed in my heart early in my life and patiently nurturing it until it blossomed into my full recovery. Thanks to Mike Likvan for helping me assemble my thoughts for this book, skilled beta reader Jacqui Likvan for cleaning up the first draft, and Danielle Swanson for her expert and honest editing. Thanks to those who helped me survive throughout my life and ordeal, especially Chris Baker, Sara Morse, Erika Horner, Aaron Marshall, and Dan Peckham. Special thanks to Mary Brewer and Chris Brewer at New Beginnings Recovery Center in Littleton, Colorado for showing me the permanent path to sobriety, Judge Jean Woodford for giving me one last chance, and Paige Lopez and her family for their continued love and support.

The Son of Man will send out his angels, and they will weed out his kingdom everything that causes sin, and all who do evil. They will throw them into the blazing furnace... Matthew 13:41-42

PART ONE

1 THE CAMPER

Friday, August eighteenth, 2017 is a day I will never forget. It started like most others but ended with me, and everything I owned, engulfed in flames. That morning I sat at a little wooden table in my pickup truck camper, minus the pickup truck, and watched sports talk shows as I mindlessly nibbled on stolen granola bars. Hourly I stepped outside my camper to suck on cigarettes. As much as I liked smoking I refused to stink up my place with the smell.

The camper where I lived was a gift from a bar friend, Sean. It was constructed of aluminum and made to fit within a pickup truck's bed. The main area was just big enough for a small table, two chairs, a mini-fridge, a tiny cabinet with a sink top, a clothes closet, a small television, and lots of little hanging air fresheners. A front compartment designed to extend over a truck cab was the sleeping area.

The camper was luxurious compared to the place I had slept in a year earlier – a large, wheelchair-accessible portable toilet in a Denver public park. Warmed with citronella candles, I used duct tape to block the toilet's vents at night. The tape kept out most of the cold night air, yet kept in all of the stench. The crisp lemony scent of the candles did nothing to mask the putrid smell that was a brutal reminder of the direction in which I'd taken my life.

I was able to upgrade to the camper when I was helping out at a bar to make some cash. Sean, one of the regulars, somehow learned I spent my nights in a portable toilet. "Dude, come live by me," he offered. "I've got an unused camper on the back of my property, sitting on an old pickup truck I never drive. It's tall enough for you to stand in and it has a separate sleeping area in the front."

He offered the camper to me because he thought I was a nice guy down on his luck. No one ever suspected I was a meth addict because I hid my addiction well. Scabs from nervous scratching, facial burns from exploding meth pipes, rotted teeth, and wrinkled, unwashed clothes were the typical appearance for those who regularly used meth. I took meticulous care of my appearance. I was mindful not to scratch any place people could see, was lucky my meth bubble rarely exploded in my face, took extra good care of my teeth, and avoided looking homeless by regularly stealing new clothes.

After several months of living on Sean's property, he told me he was selling his house and we needed to move my camper home off of his property. Another friend generously offered a concrete pad on the side of his garage where I could park the camper with power provided by a long extension cord strung from the garage. The house was on a corner lot. A road ran along the side of the house and garage giving me easier access to unload the camper. Sean let me use his pickup truck to move the camper from his property to that concrete pad.

Though the camper was an upgrade from living in the toilet, its thin metal walls with poorly constructed seams did only a slightly better job of insulating me from the Colorado winters. During the coldest nights, a borrowed space heater fought the frigid air entering through gaps in the walls to keep the place barely above freezing.

Denver's winter temperatures can fluctuate between the 70s to below zero, with daily averages hovering between the 30s and 40s. The high altitude and generous sunshine made the daytime temperatures tolerable, but after sunset, the higher altitude also caused a more drastic drop in temperatures. It was after enduring some bitterly cold nights that I decided to seal the camper's leaky joints.

My plan for sealing the camper was to get gallon buckets of black rubberized paste at a local department store to cover the camper walls. It was advertised all the time on TV as being a great sealant. I reasoned that painting the complete outside and inside with this shiny spreadable rubber would add two layers of insulation and seal the camper airtight. Plus, the black color could attract the sun during the day and warm the insides.

At the time, a bicycle and public transportation were how I got around. I did most of my shopping at that department store because it was within walking distance and had all the essentials I needed: hardware, clothes, medicine, groceries, and most importantly, poor security. I easily stole items from there and walked out undetected. If I needed a lot, I'd wait until it was busy, fill a shopping cart, and walk out the front door. I'd keep walking until I made my way back to the camper. Sometimes store employees caught me leaving and I'd abandon my cart, but many times I succeeded. Eventually, the collection of empty shopping carts outside my camper grew to a half-dozen. The other store I regularly shopped at was a bike ride and light rail train ride away. It was a long trip but well worth it to grab small but expensive electronic items that I traded at the local pawn shops when money got low.

Smearing gallons of rubber onto the camper took some effort, but meth helped manufacture the energy to complete the weeks of work. When finished, the black rubber-coated camper resembled something owned by Darth Vader. My methed-up mind thought it looked cool. More importantly, the rubber coating gave my space heater a fighting chance.

My true motivation for making the camper more bearable was my young son, Tanner. I loved being with him and wanted to show his mom, and the courts, that I could provide a good place for him to stay on the weekends I had him. I'd let Tanner sleep in my bed while I pulled all-nighters on meth.

Without a regular job, the highlight of any day was enjoying my stash of free meth, courtesy of my girlfriend's supplier. To greet the morning I grabbed my glass meth pipe and lighter, sprinkled the blue-white crystal rocks into its hole, and melted them with the flame. Once the molten meth coated the inside of the bubble, I put the pipe in my mouth and heated it again to coax the drug into a vapor I inhaled. Smoking the drug was the quickest way for me to get its high. I could have injected it, but I refused to stick myself with needles. Getting my high from the glass pipe worked fine.

Each hit was an adventure. Too much heat from the lighter and the glass end would explode, sending glass shards and molten meth into my face. Despite the danger, however, that Friday morning I took the chance to extend my drug-induced awakened state that had lasted an entire month, interrupted by the occasional cat naps forced on me by exhaustion. I was awake so much over the last four weeks that Tanner slept in my bed more than I did. The smoking continued throughout that day. By evening the sun and temperatures dropped in unison. Midsummer winds off the Rockie mountains rattled the windows. I sat at the little wooden table, lit up another bubble of meth, and enjoyed the euphoric apathy meth provided. As the meth constricted my blood vessels I felt a chill. I turned on the space heater and leaned back to enjoy the high that crept into my brain. Inside the dimly lit camper, the last bit of natural light from the windows was replaced by the fluorescent orange glow from the heater's coils. I savored the high and the warmth on my legs.

For a moment I thought about what I had said to my mom on our call the night before. *Was I serious? Had the burden of my dismal life finally gotten to the point that I considered ending it?* The noise of the rattling windows brought me back to the present and my meth brain convinced me that everything would be just fine.

I reached for some snacks out of habit. Meth suppressed my appetite but the thought of salty chips sounded appealing. I turned on my stolen TV and settled in for another all-nighter of watching whatever scratchy signals its rabbit ears delivered. Looking at the tiny television screen my thoughts drifted back to the painful memory of my eighth Christmas when I received a huge TV from my father.

2 CHRISTMAS GIFT

Bennington, Vermont was a charming town just a couple hours' drive from either Boston, New York City, or Montreal. Historically it's known as the site of a pivotal battle in America's Revolutionary War. To me, it was my charming and neighborly hometown, so small that everyone knew each other.

Around Thanksgiving, Bennington's main street became a winter wonderland of Christmas lights and decorations. That was also the time my mom started decorating the inside of our trailer. By Christmastime, every inch of our little home was wallpapered with colorful trimmings and tiny blinking lights. Even though she was a single mom who often scraped for grocery money, each Christmas she traditionally purchased a fresh tree and an abundance of presents for me and my older half-brother Tyler.

Mom developed her love for the holiday from her mother who annually hosted a festive Christmas Eve celebration for the three of us and my uncle's family. Grandma Nanny's trailer was much larger and able to accommodate everyone. She worked two jobs which afforded her the means to spoil us with food and gifts. It was fun visiting with my cousins, and my Nan prepared a culinary feast. With a steady stream of Christmas songs playing in the background, she assembled seemingly endless trays of appetizers, meats, cheeses, and desserts for us to enjoy. Her menus varied from year to year, but one traditional dish she always served was her "little smokies" – marinated mini-hotdogs in a smoky-sweet sauce. We used toothpicks to nab them from the bowl. They were my favorite. She'd warn me as she brought out the family-sized bowl, "Now, Travis, save some for the rest of the family!" Then she'd laugh her special laugh. I couldn't eat them fast enough.

Once Nan made sure everyone was sufficiently stuffed, we gathered around her Christmas tree to open gifts. Nanny's generosity was boundless. She bought us much-needed shoes and clothes, and also made sure to include a fun toy for each of us grandkids. Everyone had a great time and Nanny told us each year, "Seeing you all so happy is the best Christmas gift I can ever receive!" She was such an angel.

Going to Nan's was only the beginning of our two-day Christmas celebration. The morning after we visited her home, my mother continued the festivities by rousing us from sleep with the smells of Christmas breakfast. Mom cooked eggs and bacon, a real upgrade from our usual cold cereals. As Tyler and I stumbled half-asleep into the kitchen she'd wake us up further by saying, "Santa came!" We'd scarf down breakfast so we could open our presents. While the colorful decorations, gifts, and memorable smells made Christmas great, I suspect my love for Christmas came from something much deeper.

Shortly after I was born my father left our family. As I grew older, I became more aware that I didn't have a dad at home like the other kids in our mobile home park. This realization caused me to develop a deep sadness. It came from my naive belief that his desertion was because of something I had done or worse yet, because of who I was. The pain of living with this belief made my young mind think my father's absence meant I was unworthy of love and attention. This hurt deeply and I constantly looked for love and attention from others to prove to myself it wasn't true.

As children, we have a limited understanding of what it means to be loved. We think that love equals affection or spoiling us with attention and gifts. Our idea of love's expressions is having someone give us what we want or being cuddled, kissed, or hugged. Not until we mature do we realize we are being shown true love when our mother chooses to carry her teen pregnancies, then works multiple jobs to provide her children a comfortable place to live, clean clothes, and full stomachs. With maturity, we realize that true love is a grandmother who keeps in close contact with her daughter so she can monitor our well-being. As loving as my mom and Nanny were, however, their loving actions didn't register as expressions of the kind of love and attention my young mind craved.

It's difficult to love yourself when you have a belief of unworthiness that inhibits you from recognizing expressions of true love directed toward you. Over time, my hurt turned to anger and my frail self-esteem turned to self-hatred. I tried to show a happy face to people so they liked me, but behind my smile simmered a self-loathing that at times bubbled up to the surface as aggression.

When I began grade school, frustration was added to the mix of emotions brewing inside me. I wanted to be a good student but my undiagnosed ADHD, dyslexia, and dysgraphia destined me to fail. Not only was it hard for me to concentrate, but when I finally managed to, the words in my lesson books were a jumble of confusing letters. The disappointment of unsuccessful attempts to keep up with my class made me feel defeated and fed my self-hatred. My behavior became more disruptive and aggressive. It gained the attention of people, but unfortunately, it was the wrong kind.

In second grade the school chalked up my aggressive behaviors to being a growing boy. They suggested I join the Mount Anthony Youth Athletic Association football league as a way to channel my misplaced energies. They welcomed me as a player because I was large and tall for my age and put me on their front line. Playing football allowed me a physical release from my pent-up anger, only demanded my concentration for short periods and didn't require a lot of reading or writing to succeed. I could learn what plays I needed to make from the coach demonstrating them or drawing plays on the whiteboard. Visual lessons were a more effective way for me to learn than spoken or written ones.

I've always had an all-or-nothing attitude toward doing things and became obsessed with football. It was something I could do well. My longing to succeed at something and hear praise motivated me. My coach's words felt like a father's encouragement and gave me short-lived confidence boosts that made me feel valuable and momentarily sedated my self-hate. But at seven years old my life couldn't be all football. I still had to tackle academics. On the playing field, I received attention for being a star player. Outside the playing field, I struggled with a distorted reality of feeling stupid and unlovable.

My shattered self-confidence demanded constant care and feeding. I looked for recognition from anyone. My mom and Nanny tried their best. Tyler stepped into the role of "man of the house" to help my mom, but he couldn't emotionally replace my missing dad. In fairness to my family, no one in my life could meet the expectations of my version of love or fulfill the quantity of attention I craved. As a young grade schooler, the only one who came closest to that fantasy was a grandfatherly gentleman figure known as Santa.

His yearly visits gave me a predictable boost to my self-worth. He was a man who attentively watched over my daily life and kept a tally of every time I was naughty or nice. And even though I felt I was more bad than good, every year his delivery of presents made me feel our tallies were mismatched and, on his list, my good actions somehow outweighed my bad. Seeing those presents under the tree gave me an overwhelming, though brief, hint I was loveable. Each time I played with the gifts he left, I was reminded they were given to me because of some goodness inside me. These delusions fueled my love for Christmas.

It was my eighth Christmas when my mom, Tyler, and I were in the middle of unwrapping Santa's gifts when we heard an unexpected pounding on the front door. Thinking it might be Nanny or a cousin, I ran over and opened the door as excitedly as opening another present. I saw a smiling man who looked somewhat familiar standing there struggling to hold a monster television. I looked over at my mom, confused why this person from her old snapshots was standing at our door.

It turns out this man was my father, an infrequently employed electrician who married his high school girlfriend after he got her pregnant with me. Shortly after my birth, he deserted us, not quite ready to stop sowing his wild oats.

I turned back to look at him and smelled the alcohol on his breath as he greeted me with, "Merry Christmas, buddy!" In that brief moment, I forgot about his absence and wanted to believe that giving me this television was his way of saying he loved me. He brought the television inside, laid it down, and attempted an awkward hug. He stayed only long enough to enjoy hearing my thanks for delivering the present. My mother said a few words – none of which were an invitation for him to stay. Then he was gone again.

At that time, my success in intramural sports fueled my obsession with professional sports. I religiously watched professional football and became a Denver Broncos fan simply because I liked their colors of blue and orange. Soon I idolized their star linebacker, Karl Mecklenburg, and their star quarterback, John

Elway. In football's off-season, I followed baseball. Vermont didn't have a professional baseball team so I had to pick between Boston's Red Sox or New York's Yankees. My brother and most of our friends rooted for the Red Sox. I chose to be different and picked the Yankees because, in the second round of the 1981 Major League Baseball's Amateur Draft, they drafted a young player named John Elway.

Having my own TV in my room allowed me to enjoy my sports obsession without monopolizing my family's TV. I cherished this gift more than any other I'd received from Santa because it made my self-loathing begin to melt away.

It was two weeks later while watching the Broncos play the Kansas City Chiefs, that I heard another unexpected knock on our trailer door. When my mom opened it there stood two young men. "Hi! We're Nick and Ray from Rent-A-Center." It was a place where people rented home furnishings. It also rented televisions. They informed my mom that my father had visited their store on Christmas Eve to rent a television for a week. It was now going on two weeks and with it not being returned, they looked up the address he gave and came to repossess it.

My mom was not surprised but my mind was reeling. I was shocked that the man who crushed my self-esteem so many years ago made a point to return with this cruel joke to remind me I didn't deserve his love. My healing came to a screeching halt as my self-hatred dug its heels deeper into my heart.

Everyone read the disappointment and shock on my face and my mom tried to lighten the mood by asking, "You boys want some sodas?" Nick and Ray agreed to the drinks and showed great compassion. They were sports fans too and distracted my mind by engaging me in talk of players and stats. My mom got us sodas and found the Broncos game on our other TV. Together they sat with me patiently watching part of the game before they excused themselves and gently removed what I believed was my television set.

I appreciated their sensitivity and sports talk so much that anytime my mom and I went grocery shopping next to their store, I stopped in to chat about football. They were always happy to give me the time. Eventually, these guys would help me find a job. But first I had to find Jesus.

3 THE JESUS SEED

By the time I became a freshman at Mount Anthony Union High School, I was well-known around Bennington. I was a mediocre student at best, but I'd become an accomplished lineman. Because of my size, I was affectionately referred to as Moose or Marshmallow by my football teammates. Driven by a deep-seated need for love and attention that lived in every fiber of my being, I'd perfected the art of generating attention and making people like me. I'd also perfected the art of hiding the self-loathing that whispered to me constantly that I wasn't good enough or deserving of anyone's attention or love.

I enjoyed my popularity but it was superficial. Those people didn't know the real me. I craved a deeper relationship. I knew Nanny loved me and so did my mom. I even felt my soon-to-be stepdad, Chris believed in me or at least shared my love of the Yankees. But they were family. I wanted a peer to accept me for the broken person I was. Someone who knew school was going to take me more years to finish than most students and didn't think I was stupid. Someone who knew I smoked pot to numb the endless unworthiness loop playing in my head, and still liked me. Someone who witnessed when my self-hatred triggered outbursts, and still believed I was a good person. I found that kind of friendship from my teammate, Joshua.

Joshua and I met at football practice and became fast friends. When I was introduced to his family, they welcomed me as another son. I spent all of my free time with Joshua and his family. When they went spin casting for muskies on the Niagara River or sightseeing in Punxsutawney, Pennsylvania, they invited me along. In the summer I worked alongside Joshua at his father's logging company. It was physically challenging but I saw it as paid exercise to build my strength for football.

Joshua's family was my first exposure to Christians and awareness of someone's religion. Growing up we never made religion a part of our life. In contrast, the people in Joshua's family were seven-day-a-week Christians who celebrated Sundays as "church day."

Every Sunday they drove to a different church to discover new uplifting expressions of Christian worship. Afterward, they selected a restaurant for lunch where they enjoyed a meal and talked about their experiences. Tagging along with them on Sundays exposed me to a spiritual side of life I didn't know existed. I learned about Jesus, the loving Son of God, and how He positively influenced people's lives. I watched how they treated Jesus as a living entity in their lives. Whenever they arrived anywhere, they prayed to Him before they exited their car. Together they said a prayer inspired by Ephesians chapter 6 verse 11, "Put on the Full Armor of God, Belt of Truth, Breastplate of Righteousness, Shield of Faith, Sword of the Spirit, Shoes of the Gospel and Helmet of Salvation." It was their way of asking Jesus to watch over them throughout their day.

I reveled in the love that flowed between them and was intrigued by their faith. Being with Joshua and his family made my inner darkness a shade lighter.

Of all the family outings I attended with them, the one that had the greatest impact on my life was the 1997 DC Talk concert with Toby Mac. It was my first music concert. Toby McKeehan, who later left the band DC Talk for a solo career where he changed his last name to Mac, was just a few years into his journey to Christian music stardom. His group played in small venues like universities and churches. As young as his career was at the time, our little town of Bennington didn't offer a venue big enough for his fans so I drove with Joshua's family to Crossroads Community Church in Amsterdam, New York.

I didn't know what to expect as we sat in the darkened church theater waiting for the concert to begin. Then through the darkness, men took the stage with helmets shooting lasers into the audience. As the beams connected with people, the crowd's anticipation and excitement grew. The stage lights sprung to life and the band erupted into their first rock song, Jesus Freak. It was reminiscent of Nirvana and everyone cheered. The music and theatrics mesmerized me and took me outside the troubled world inside my head.

Halfway through the concert, Toby walked to the front of the stage to address the audience. The house lights brightened and he talked about Jesus' unconditional love and the promises He makes to anyone who commits to being His follower. Toby explained that commitment required a conscious decision to welcome Jesus into our hearts. Knowing how Jesus influenced Joshua's family, Toby's words connected with me. He invited anyone who was interested to come up to the stage and make that commitment to accept Jesus into their hearts. I turned to look at Joshua's family. They were all looking at me, wondering how I'd react to Toby's invitation. My smile told them I was thinking of going to Toby and they encouraged me. I joined the line of people waiting to reach the stage.

When I got to Toby, he gave me a Bible. I held it tightly as he gently put his hand on my head and prayed, "Jesus, enter this young man's heart and bring him your peace." His loving touch planted the seed of Jesus within me.

Unfortunately, that seed landed on a hardened surface and I would confound its attempts to sprout by keeping it in the shadow of bad decisions and drug abuse for the next two decades. Its ability to ever grow inside me was impossible. Fortunately, God likes accomplishing the impossible.

4 DRUG OF CHOICE

The first of my three years as a high school senior was a pivotal year for me. Most of my classmates were graduating, including my friend Joshua. While I still needed more credits to graduate, he was headed off to college, weakening my connection to him, his family, and Christianity.

I could have graduated high school with the rest of my class if I were given school credits for being the class clown, the friend who looked old enough to buy alcohol, the popular druggy who always had weed or a wild man on the football field. I neglected my academics and invested all my energy in seeking popularity to quiet my wounded self-esteem. I also grew my football skills, believing they might be my ticket out of Bennington. I saw football players as the ultimate success story. They enjoyed worldwide popularity and million-dollar paychecks. I idolized John Elway. I wanted to be him. Most days in high school I wore an Elway jersey and was thrilled when my classmates nicknamed me Elway. John Elway was such an idol that for my senior yearbook I found a picture of him in a suit and put that photo in place of mine in the book. Deep down I wanted to be anyone but the unlovable me. I saw becoming a successful sports star like Elway as the ultimate way to avenge my father and make him regret ever abandoning me.

During my high school years, the voice of my childish belief of unworthiness became deafening. Pot temporarily numbed its relentless taunting, but popularity became my drug of choice. The notoriety I had in my little town made me feel vindicated against the monster inside my head telling me no one would ever love me. Superficially, the attention I got proved to my inner child's mind that I was indeed loveable.

Along with seeking popularity came greed. I became my own Santa, showering myself with gifts as reminders that I was deserving of nice things. My greed demanded instant and constant gratification. I needed to find a steady source of income to feed it so I found a job as a stock boy at a new office supply store in town called Staples.

I saved my first few paychecks and bought a used Audi 500. It was a boxy sedan, but to me, it was freedom and another step toward adulthood. I also bought a vanity license plate with the letters MR ELWAY. With a good job, a car, and dreams of a football career, graduating high school became a low priority. My life outside of high school had already started and not having a diploma didn't hinder me.

Driven by the desire to buy more material items, I put in as many hours as I could at Staples. They misinterpreted my greed as dedication and rewarded me with a promotion to management.

It's a funny practice businesses have when it comes to picking managers. It's usually the hardest worker who moves to that position. But being a worker and being a manager are two different skill sets. It's like taking a good football lineman and promoting him to coach because he had the most quarterback sacks. Playing great on the field doesn't translate to having the skills and strategies needed to coach all the players in their various positions. Nonetheless, they foolishly gave this hardworking stock boy the keys to the store.

As my greed grew, it became harder to spoil myself with meager weekly paychecks. I had a nice car, but I wanted to upgrade it with an impressive stereo. I'd seen one at the Berkshire Mall in Lanesborough for about $400. Now that I was spending wildly, saving that much money would take forever! I needed to find some quick cash and came up with a plan.

Nobody locked their doors in the mobile home park where I lived. In my sleepy little town, everyone knew everyone and trust was a value in our community that everyone shared. But I knew this open-door policy was my ticket to a new car stereo. I remembered that the older couple next door usually left their checkbook out on the kitchen counter. I was certain they wouldn't miss one check.

Here was the problem with my plan. From all outward appearances, I looked like an adult. At seventeen I was tall with a beard. But inside, my brain belonged to a seventeen-year-old. Right behind every seventeen-year-old's forehead is the brain's prefrontal cortex. It is this part of the brain that helps people think through the potential consequences of their actions. It doesn't fully develop until it's about twenty-five years old. This is why car insurance rates drop when a person turns twenty-five. It's the point when their matured prefrontal cortex finally helps them become a more cautious driver.

So, while my outside looked like a fully developed adult, the part of my brain that would make me think twice about stealing a check wasn't quite doing its job yet.

Armed with my plan, I visited my neighbors and ripped off one of their checks. I then wrote the check for cash, signed their name to it, and had a classmate who worked at the local grocery store cash it. My plan went flawlessly.

But my hunger for material goods wasn't satisfied with getting a new stereo. I wanted more things to satisfy my greedy hunger pangs of unworthiness. A Staples coworker and I devised a plan to collect free gaming CDs. We purchased the CDs at a local gaming store, removed the discs, and replaced them with blanks, then used the shrink wrap machine at Staples to make it look like the packaging was never opened. We then returned them and got our money back and collected lots of free gaming CDs. We were brilliant!

Accumulating things appeased my greed. Having a steady stream of cash made me more popular. As I neared my eighteenth birthday, everyone who knew me was excited to wish me well on my birthday – except for two.

5 BIRTHDAY GIFT

On the last remaining days of my seventeenth year, I was on top of the world. My manager's job and schemes were netting me nice things and enough money to pay for my car and an apartment. When I wasn't working or partying with friends, I was enjoying continued success as a high school football player. I was dating a cute coworker from Staples and my popularity in the town was at an all-time high. I had a few run-ins with Bennington police, but they were minor teenage offenses like underage drinking or Halloween pranks with raw eggs. Fortunately, my notoriety and likeability usually got me off with little more than a slap on the wrist.

I decided to throw myself a party to celebrate my milestone birthday. Finally, at eighteen I would be my own man who could make my own decisions and be recognized as responsible. I would no longer be considered a child.

Being recognized as an adult, particularly in the eyes of the law, is exactly why the morning I turned eighteen, two uniformed officers showed up on my doorstep. Instead of wishing me a happy birthday, they said, "Travis Morse? We have a warrant for your arrest."

It turns out that when my neighbors discovered a year earlier someone had forged one of their checks, they filed a police report that initiated an investigation. Fairly quickly the police determined I was the culprit, but they dragged their feet in arresting me because they knew as a juvenile the punishment for my crime would be minor. They waited until my eighteenth birthday to arrest me as an adult.

Bennington was such a small town they didn't handcuff me or throw me in jail, they simply told me to appear the next day in court. At that hearing, the judge charged me with False Pretense and sentenced me to nine months in Marble Valley Regional Correctional Center. I was lucky. Had my greed been a little greater I could have been charged with Grand Theft, spent up to 3 years in prison, and forever more been labeled a convicted felon.

After sentencing me, the judge gave me a week to get my things in order. I spoke to the couple whose check I stole. I was such a likable guy they apologized to me for filing a police report. They said had they known it was me they would have settled the matter privately.

When my mom found out about the sentence she organized a goodbye barbecue so family and friends could see me off. Everyone I knew came to wish me well except for Nanny who at this point was bedridden with cancer.

Next to my mom, Nanny was my favorite person in the whole world. She was sweet, generous, and a little quirky. Whereas most of her older generation listened to news radio to keep up on current events, Nanny's source of local news was a police scanner. If someone in town was stopped by the Bennington Police she knew about it first.

Before she was homebound, whenever our families got together for picnics or parties, she'd take me aside and ask, "What's this I heard about you being stopped by the police?" Then she'd wink and tell me, "Behave yourself." Whatever she knew about my brushes with the law she kept our little secret. Sadly, as much as she cared about me, her loving concern just couldn't penetrate my hardened belief of being unlovable.

Visiting my sick Nan before I started serving my sentence was important to me. She had been fighting breast cancer on and off for fifteen years and was losing her battle. I visited her at her mobile home and we had a wonderful talk. Despite her dire condition, she was surprisingly upbeat. As we said our goodbyes I wondered, *Is she going to die before I finish serving my sentence?* The thought made my eyes tear. I held her hand and didn't want to leave. She read the question in my eyes and sweetly promised me, "I'll wait for you."

Life in the correctional center was a wake-up call. No longer did I have the freedom to do what I wanted and with whomever I wanted. I was socially removed from my friends and my favorite regular customers at Staples. I was isolated from the life I knew. Some of the inmates were acquaintances from town, but being around them wasn't any consolation.

The upside to being in jail is it forced me to clean myself up. I got three square meals a day and I had nothing to do with my time but sit and think, and read. I brought the Bible I got from Toby Mac and I sat and read it. I was drawn to the book of Proverbs. In its first five verses it describes its value:

> *"The proverbs of Solomon son of David, king of Israel: for gaining wisdom and instruction; for understanding words of insight; for receiving instruction in prudent behavior, doing what is right and just and fair; for giving prudence to those who are simple, knowledge and discretion to the young- let the wise listen and add to their learning, and let the discerning get guidance."*

Proverbs has 31 chapters so I used it as a daily inspiration. I'd pick whatever chapter coincided with the day of the month, read that chapter, then think about it. In a small way, it fed the Jesus seed trying to grow within my heart.

As much as the jail was good for me, I still longed to get back to the life I knew. Before I went to jail, my girlfriend broke up with me, so when I needed to hear a friendly voice, I made a collect call to my mom. She always took my calls. One time when we talked, my mom told me that Nanny had started a letter-writing campaign petitioning the courts to grant me an early release. She flooded the court with letters but progress was slow and Nan didn't have much strength or time. My mom stepped in and drove to see my parole officer. She explained the relationship between me and Nan and said my life would be forever damaged if Nan died before I got out of jail. The courts agreed to commute my sentence from six months served to one year of house arrest. Freedom at last!

In some ways, house arrest was more restrictive than the correctional center. I had an ankle monitor so my location was always tracked. Before I could see someone, I had to get the approval of the court. If the court agreed to let me have a visitor, the length of the visit was limited. Most of my friends didn't bother jumping through those hoops.

My parent's house became my new prison and theirs. They had to remove any guns or alcohol from the house. A law enforcement officer, parole officer, or probation officer could visit anytime without notice and do an intrusive inspection to look for violations. The only time I could leave their property was to go to work. Thankfully, Staples held my job for me while I was incarcerated. The house arrest guidelines didn't allow me to drive my car without scrutinizing each trip, so I rode my bike to work. The monotonous isolation of house arrest was in deep contrast to the social life I enjoyed before my arrest. But the part that bothered me the most wasn't being confined or not getting to see my friends, it was not seeing my Nanny. She had initiated a writing campaign to help get me out of prison and I wasn't able to visit her to look her in the eyes and thank her.

What's even worse is during all of this my Nanny's condition worsened. Her failing health was constantly on my mind. I didn't normally pray, but knowing that Joshua's family believed prayer worked and my Nanny was very near death, I prayed to Jesus on my bike rides to and from work to please let me see her one last time. It was one morning on my way to Staples that He answered my prayers.

During that ride, my bike cable mysteriously snapped and got entangled in the wheel's spokes. The bike stopped abruptly and threw me face-first onto the pavement. Some people saw the accident and called

911. I don't remember much as I kept going in and out of consciousness. When I finally awoke I was in a hospital bed with bruises, a concussion, a dislocated shoulder, and missing half of the skin from my face that I left on the pavement. My body hurt more than it ever did after a football game.

While in bed trying to make sense of what had happened, the nurse come in to check on the patient next to me. Listening to their conversation from behind the privacy curtain I heard a very familiar voice. It was Nanny! Jesus had found a way to get me free of house arrest long enough to see her again.

I struggled to get out of bed and went over to her. My face was so road rashed at first she didn't recognize me. She was weak and I stood next to her bed holding her hand. I thanked her for the writing campaign. She whispered, "You've always been my favorite, Travis. I just couldn't let you suffer." I sat there in silence thinking about what she said.

Soon we both were released. I went back to my parent's home and in two weeks she died at her home and went back to Jesus. After that, anytime I thought of the bike accident I smiled, thankful that Jesus arranged that moment for me and my Nanny.

6 SELF-SABOTAGE

Midway through my nineteenth year, my house arrest ended and the sting of the whole ordeal quickly waned. By then I'd abandoned any hope of a high school diploma or a football career. I was content making money, re-establishing my circle of friends, and seeing my mom happy with my step-dad. I was finally out of their hair and back in an apartment. I earned a raise and a new love interest at Staples. Life was going better than I thought I deserved.

Having a life this good disturbed my ingrained belief of unworthiness. Like the rented TV at Christmas, I thought these good things needed to be taken away so reality could once again fall in line with my beliefs.

Deep-seated beliefs are powerful controllers of our life. Established early on by our naïve minds, they form the ground on which we grow our lives. Unless we step back at some point and examine the accuracy of these beliefs, they allow roots to grow deeper and feed whatever blooms as a result. My young mind planted a self-image based on the dismal beliefs that I was unlovable and unworthy of good things. I never examined the validity of these beliefs and they grew stronger and deeper. By nineteen, they became adult beliefs with a stranglehold on my life's decisions.

Any well-adjusted person could see how my life contradicted my subconscious beliefs. They could recognize that I had friends, a loving family, and a girlfriend proving I was deserving of love. They could point to me earning a management position and my employer holding my job while I was incarcerated to demonstrate I deserved good things. They could see all of these successes as indications I was both lovable and worthy of goodness.

But I wasn't well-adjusted. My twisted self-image distorted my beliefs. When reality contradicted those beliefs, my attitude was reality must be fixed to correct the mismatch. The only way to do this was for me to sabotage my successes.

That is why, when Staples gave me control over the inventory, instead of being responsible, I decided to use it to my advantage. I realized I could sell computer equipment out the back door, make easy cash, get incredible discounts for my friends, and modify the inventory records so the stolen products disappeared. My disturbed self-image devised a plan that would get me fired and help reality once again realign with my negative beliefs of what I deserved.

My sabotage worked. I was only able to sneak out about $2,600 in products before an independent auditor discovered discrepancies in the inventory. All fingers pointed at me and Staples fired me. But instead of pressing charges, my likeability let me avoid any involvement with the law and Staples asked me to simply pay back the $2,600. I turned to Joshua's father for the money with the promise I would work it off at his logging company. He agreed.

Because of my crime, I lost my job, my income, my apartment, and my girlfriend. At twenty years old I was back with my parents and living the disappointing life I imagined I deserved. Word spread that I was out of a job, though fortunately no one knew the reason why. My friends Nick and Ray got me a job at Rent-A-Center.

After work, I started hanging out at a popular bar owned by my old football coach. He let me make some extra money helping the bartenders keep the bar stocked. That place became my social life. For a broken young man who was at the mercy of his abusive inner voices, cozying up with this bar crowd was another in a series of very bad ideas.

7 OUT OF LUCK

Murphy's Tavern was *the* local hangout for the townies of Bennington. Patrons were a mixture of adults and teenagers who congregated to play pool. They didn't deny entrance to people under twenty-one until the town's evening curfew started. The place was much like the television bar Cheers minus the ambiance, charm, humor, or floor space, and with a lot more regulars. Many of them were my former classmates; others were people I'd seen around town. Most didn't come to socialize as much as to drown their sorrows. I related to them because my life's disappointments mirrored many of theirs.

Whereas customers at Rent-A-Center engaged me in upbeat conversations about their lives, the conversations around Murphy's centered on despair, disappointment, and depression. Hanging out there after work exposed me to the underbelly of the town. Most were smokers and I took up their habit to fit in.

My bar buddies were driven by the same negative self-talk that attracted me to that dump. But in other ways, it was fun being there. Some were my old classmates who still called me Elway, and when we weren't wallowing in self-pity, we were talking sports and cheering at the games on the TVs.

Helping out at Murphy's as a barback took little time or brainpower so I spent most of my time socializing and playing pool. Even though I could steal a free buzz by sneaking a swig or two of liquor from the bottles that I brought up from the storage closet to replenish the bar, I didn't need to. Most times I was already high on weed before I arrived at Murphy's.

One regular, Billy, noticed how the whites of my eyes often looked like roadmaps and asked about my drug use. I wrote him off as nosey. I didn't realize he was trying to engage me in conversation so he could offer me something stronger.

Drugs were easy to get in my hometown and for the most part, law enforcement looked the other way. As long as the citizens weren't hurting each other, they turned a blind eye to minor offenses.

Billy was a heavy recreational drug user but didn't broadcast that fact. One night when the bar was fairly empty, Billy came in to shoot some pool and engage me in our usual mindless chatting. He excused himself and went to the bathroom. When he returned I noticed a residue of white powder in his nostrils. I asked, "Did you just do coke?" He gave me a wry smile. The effects of the drug on him didn't seem too drastic and I asked if he'd let me try some. He slipped me a small baggie. I grabbed a straw from the bar and went into the bathroom to try it. The high was like a shot of adrenaline! My mind cleared, my energy rose and I was ultra-focused on the activities around the bar. I looked at Billy wide-eyed and said, "I like this!" Billy laughed because he knew what I was feeling and he motioned for me to wipe my nose.

After that, Billy sold me cocaine periodically and introduced me to many different recreational drugs including mescaline, Ecstacy, LSD, opium, and mushrooms. Each had a different high. The smoothest was Ecstacy; the craziest was LSD. Somewhere in between were mushrooms.

The first time I tried mushrooms I wasn't at Murphy's, fortunately, because the high included hallucinations. I don't think I would have been able to function as a barback or even a pool player with my mind in that condition.

Billy's collection of recreational drugs was a great distraction from my monotonous life, but their effects didn't last. When I came down from my high I still had to face the reality that my life in Bennington was boring and unrewarding. My popularity around town was waning and genuine relationships were few. My bar friendships were superficial and my love lives consisted of empty-headed party girls who hung out at Murphy's.

I was losing connection with my family. My Nanny was gone and my older brother whom I respected and admired tremendously had moved to Colorado. The only relative left in Bennington was my "grandma" Mary, a sweet woman whom we'd visit once in a while. She treated me like her grandson even though technically, she was the mom of Tyler's dad. My mom and stepdad were still around, but I didn't want to interfere with their life together, so drugs became my favorite companions. Billy kept me supplied with a variety of them and I became skilled at being a highly functional drug user. Well, most of the time.

One night I ingested mushrooms after leaving Murphy's. I don't know where I was heading and as high as I was, I probably didn't care. I stopped at an intersection and waited for the light to change. After sitting there for what felt like just a moment, flashing lights appeared in my rearview mirror. I noticed the traffic light was green and drove through the intersection and pulled over to the curb. The officer said, "I pulled you over because you didn't proceed when the light turned green, twice. Please show me your license, registration, and proof of insurance." By my slow clumsy movements, he could tell I was either high on something or having a stroke. He asked me to step out of the car. I felt off-balanced. Other officers showed up and the car was searched. They found lots of drugs and I was taken into custody to go before a judge the next day.

Sitting in the holding cell, I decided I was done with Bennington. My notoriety was changing from popular townie to local has-been. At almost twenty-one, I was no longer going to enjoy a slap on the wrist from the police for my bad boy antics. My luck in Bennington had run out.

In court the next day the stone-faced judge read the charges to me. "Travis Morse, you're charged with driving while under the influence, possession of illegal substances, and driving less than the posted speed. How do you plead?" It was obvious they were throwing the book at me and didn't want to see my face in that courtroom ever again.

I turned on all my charm and threw myself at the mercy of the court. "Your Honor," I pleaded, "I realize I screwed up. Can you please give me another chance? I'll straighten up. And if you let me go I'll pack up my things and move away from Vermont."

The judge, hearing that Bennington law enforcement could finally rid itself of me, agreed to let me go provided I was out of the state by the end of the month, stayed out of trouble until then, and refrained from using drugs for the remainder of my stay in town. I promised to do all three. I did the first two.

It was time for me to leave Vermont and start a completely new life. I talked to my brother about my need for a change. He told me I could live with him temporarily, but that I'd need to get my life together and find a job when I got to Colorado. Nick and Ray's manager supported my transfer to a Colorado Rent-A-Center.

My neglected Audi couldn't survive the cross-country trip so for Christmas my brother and mom bought me a Greyhound bus ticket for the two-day trip to Colorado. I was hopeful this move would be a fresh start. My brother was a responsible young man and his friends would be my new social group. I believed moving across the country would help me leave my demons behind. My demons had other plans.

PART TWO

8 LONG, STRANGE TRIP

Greyhound tries to make their buses comfortable and safe, but can't pick and choose their passengers. My two-day trip from Vermont to Colorado was like a rolling bad neighborhood and the portion from Chicago to Colorado got downright bizarre.

Around 5 AM my mom drove me to the bus stop in Bennington which was nothing more than a row of covered benches. They were in a parking lot behind a small two-story building with windows and white siding that looked like it might have been a home at one point. The sun was just rising as we sat there on that chilly December morning waiting. My mom repeatedly reminded me that she hoped I would be safe and happy in Colorado. Each time she spoke her voice cracked and her lip quivered more. I understood her sadness. Soon both of her sons would be living far away from her.

I tried to act stoic, but I also felt sad about leaving a woman who loved me so dearly. My eyes welled up with tears as the bus approached. I picked up my backpack and two suitcases and she hugged me hard, not wanting to let me leave, but we both knew it was the best thing for me to do.

The bus driver got out and wished us a good morning, then grabbed my suitcases and tucked them into the belly of his bus. I kept my backpack with me. It had the essentials I'd need for the two-day trip; some snacks, a carton of cigarettes, a dozen mini-liquor bottles, and a going-away present from Billy -- an ounce of weed, ten joints, five Percocet, and five Vicodin. When he handed me the bundle he told me, "The Percocet will help you sleep and the Vicodin will reduce the pain of having to take a two-day bus ride to Colorado!" We laughed.

The bus was fairly empty. I was a little paranoid about everything I had in the backpack so I picked a seat in the back corner of the bus across from the bathroom and popped a Percocet. I'd already smoked a joint before I got on the bus so I sat back, closed my eyes, and hoped the drugs would let me stay asleep until we got to Colorado. Regrettably, my paranoia interrupted my napping and by the first stop, I was ready for another dose of something.

The first stop was Albany, New York. We had an hour-and-a-half layover while the driver transferred our belongings to another bus. I walked around the bus station to stretch my legs and clutched my backpack while I lit a cigarette. One of the other passengers approached me. He lifted his chin with a jerking motion and said, "Hey." I responded with a simple, "Hi," suspicious as to why this guy approached me. It turns out he could smell the weed on my clothes and wanted to share a joint. He seemed okay, so I agreed. Then he held out his hand and said, "I'm John." I shook his hand and replied, "Travis." Maybe the trip wouldn't be so bad after all.

The next stop was New York City and again we had a long layover while we switched buses and lost and gained passengers. John and I extended our high with more weed and polished off some of my mini-liquor bottles. At the next stop, Harrisburg, Pennsylvania, we shared another joint. Traveling with John was making the trip somewhat bearable.

When we got to the Pittsburgh stop, my paranoia kicked into high gear. As we approached the bus station, there were multiple vehicles with flashing lights on top. *Someone found out about my backpack and called the DEA! Those drug enforcement agents are waiting to ambush me once the bus arrives.* I calmed a bit as we got closer because I noticed a paramedic van along with a mixture of police cars and fire trucks. Someone had died at the bus stop shortly before we arrived. Even still, I left my backpack hidden on the floor by my seat and only ventured a few feet from the bus to stretch my legs and have a cigarette.

The next stop was Cleveland, Ohio and we swapped buses again. Sadly I said goodbye to my travel partner, John. Cleveland had a cool vibe about it, much like John. We shared his last joint and I promised myself I'd return to Cleveland someday.

I took a nap on the seven-hour journey from Cleveland to South Bend, Indiana. I woke as we entered the station and had just enough time for a cigarette and a joint before we were off to Chicago, Illinois. That is where Chicken Lady got on.

She was a feisty woman with inner-city anger and a large cloth shopping bag filled with buckets of Kentucky Fried Chicken. While we stood in line to get on the bus, someone walked through the line and accidentally kicked her shopping bag. She let loose with a tirade of expletives and threatened the life of the very apologetic person who did it.

On the bus, she needed two seats for the trip. She sat in the window seat and the aisle seat was taken up by her shopping bag filled with chicken.

I admit, when we first got on the bus her fried chicken smelled like a perfect recipe for my munchies. I was pretty stoned by then. Unfortunately the scent of that chicken, and the noises she made while eating it, quickly got old.

She sat by herself and spoke to no one. Maybe it was because her mother taught her not to talk with her mouth full; which it was for the remainder of the trip to Colorado. She went through piece after piece of that chicken, plunking the bones into the cardboard buckets after emptying each one. The sound reverberated throughout the bus each time.

When we got to Des Moines, the second stop in

Iowa, the bus driver was replaced by another. I think he was already scheduled to end his shift, but it wouldn't surprise me if he called ahead and asked Greyhound to get him out of this bus because of the smell of the fried chicken and the sound of the bones clunking in the buckets.

Chicken Lady slowly worked through the pieces and threw out one of the buckets of bones at the request of the driver when we got to our third stop in Nebraska.

By the time we entered Colorado, the tasty smell of fresh fried chicken was long gone, replaced by the greasy odor of chicken parts left in her buckets. I'd already smoked a few more joints, finished the liquor bottles, most of the Vicodin, and two of the Percocet. The drugs helped me sleep through most of her eating. I woke as the bus entered the Denver area to witness the rising sun reflected off of the Rocky Mountains. It was like a dream.

When we arrived at Union Station in downtown Denver I was supposed to call my brother to drive me back to his place in the suburbs, but seeing the city across the street from the station, I just had to explore. Denver was so different from the single main street in Bennington with craft shops, secondhand clothing stores, and antiques that I'd left in Bennington. With each new street I walked I became more impressed, but also more anxious to see my brother.

I called Tyler and headed back to Union Station. On the way back I thought about my past: my stealing, being in jail, and my excessive drug use. I hoped all that remained in the past. I was excited to restart my life in this bigger city with my brother and find opportunities to make my life better. My destructive demons were also excited by the prospect of finding bigger city opportunities to screw up my life.

9 YOU CAN'T HIDE

My brother was excited to have me near. He organized a get-together with some of his buddies who were our Bennington friends that had also moved to Colorado. We went to an upscale bar and restaurant called C.B. & Potts in Westminster. It was nice to bond with them again and watch sports together over dinner and beers.

As we drank, I learned what everyone had been doing since they left Bennington and that getting drunk was much easier in the higher altitudes of Denver. Even though I maintained my usual pace of drinking, the altitude accelerated the effect and I quickly became hammered. By morning, I also learned the drier air in Colorado accelerated the dehydrating effect of the alcohol. I woke with a killer hangover and cotton mouth like I'd never experienced. I wasted the entire day drinking water and hoping to die.

That was a hint that Denver was not Bennington and I learned a powerful lesson about moderation. I acted like a Boy Scout for about a month. Cigarettes, weed, and maybe a few light beers were the extent of my vices. Part of my reason for wanting to be good was the memory of that night of drinking. Another part was that my brother knew very little about my problems in Vermont. He knew I had minor brushes with the law but was unaware of my heavy recreational drug use, and my mom never told him about me stealing from Staples. Being around him and his friends made it easier for me to behave myself.

Living in Denver was a literal breath of fresh air. I loved being near my brother and his Colorado buddies. They were outstanding young men. One was who I bought my Audi from in Bennington. He worked at a car dealership in Colorado and helped me find another car. It was a '98 Honda Civic and he had the dealer's service department make sure it was in great shape for me. My brother cosigned for my car loan.

Being with my brother improved my life. I was around a better circle of friends, had a good job at Rent-A-Center, and had a reliable car. As I settled into Colorado, a coworker, Damon, offered to take me downtown to explore more of the city's bustling nightlife. I remember when we walked into our first bar. It was packed and the energy was exhilarating!

Damon and I had a few beers and quickly lost track of each other in the crowd. I'm not sure where he went but I ended up charming my way into a bar-hopping bachelorette party. Making new friends was easy because I was blessed with a charisma that instantly made people attracted to me, especially women. Usually the wrong women.

After about the third or fourth bar, one of the more wild girls from the party met up with a friend of hers. He was a former boxer who'd come to join the party. He and I tried to carry on a conversation but it was so noisy we went outside where we could hear each other better. His Cadillac was parked right in front. He suggested we sit in it instead of standing on the sidewalk. Immediately he asked, "Do you wanna do a bump?" I knew it was an invitation to snort cocaine. Having fuzzy judgment from an alcohol-soaked brain, I agreed. He pressed a button on his console that flipped open a door. Out slid a motorized tray with baggies of coke. It was surreal and I thought, *I've traveled almost 2,000 miles across the country to get away from drugs, and yet they found me!* My demons had succeeded in leading me right back to what I hoped to escape.

That's the thing about our demons. We can run, but we can't hide because they live inside us. They follow us wherever we go and influence our behavior. Until we identify them and find out what they're feeding on, these parasites will tirelessly suck the goodness out of our lives. As much as I wondered why my life kept turning to shambles, I still had no clue it was my childhood traumas that drove my poor decisions and made me easy prey to whatever or whoever offered temporary relief from my internal pain.

The ex-boxer and I did the first hit of cocaine and my world went blank. It resumed hours later and a hundred miles away when I woke up alone lying on the hard ground beneath a sign that read "Welcome To Pueblo, Colorado."

I grabbed my cell phone and called Damon. I explained that I drank too much and ended up in Pueblo. He brought me back to my brother's place. Outwardly to my brother, I pretended I was out all night having fun. Inside I was beating myself up that I couldn't resist jumping right back into the quagmire of illegal drug use.

10 GATEWAY

After my adventure in Denver, I kept my intoxicants to an occasional beer and weed. I kept drinking because it was something I did socially with my brother and friends and smoking weed had been an integral part of my life since I was fifteen.

During my sabbatical from hard drugs, I went to work, spent time with my brother and his friends, and partied once in a while with Damon. I succeeded in staying away from any drugs other than marijuana for about a year and a half. What I didn't realize is if I was going to ever quit the hard drugs completely, I needed to avoid *all* drugs. As long as weed was a part of my daily life, it was going to be a gateway to those other drugs.

Some will claim that weed won't lead to harder drugs. People who smoke marijuana regularly, commonly called "stoners," will tell you all they want to do is smoke weed and have no desire to do anything harder. I'm here to argue that its gateway properties are not the drug itself, but the lifestyle.

Marijuana users live a lifestyle influenced by the sedating effects of that drug. And while people who drink alcohol also experience similar effects, most people who drink don't roll out of bed and mix a cocktail, whereas stoners proudly joke about the "wake & bake" process for starting their day.

Weed users start their day adopting a laissez-faire attitude toward life. They invite cloudy thinking that decreases their desires, and motivation, and increases their willingness to accept lower standards of conduct and morals. Stoners associate with like-minded people along the fringes of society. They welcome people of lower standards into their circle of friends because these are the only people who want to be in that circle.

Weed weakens people's defenses. It makes them susceptible to ignoring danger signs in situations and relationships, signs that sober-thinking people recognize as something they should avoid. Sober thinking provides clarity for seeing certain situations and relationships as foolish, unproductive, or potentially harmful. Thanks to my continued weed use, I didn't have that clarity.

Living with Tyler and hanging out with his friends influenced my behaviors positively. Being away from my Bennington buddies also helped me act more responsibly at my job. But while living under the influence of my brother kept me out of trouble, this new life was boring. I woke up, went to work, hung out with my brother and friends, and smoked weed to medicate my internal pain. My life had no meaning. Like Viktor Frankl said, "When a person can't find a deep sense of meaning, they distract themselves with pleasure." That's what my life lacked – meaning and some good old-fashioned, irresponsible pleasure.

My brother wanted the best for me but with him around I couldn't have the kind of fun I wanted. I decided to move out of his place and in with Damon. He was renting a house and wouldn't scrutinize my actions. This move took me away from the watchful eyes of my brother and the positive influence of his friends.

11 WATERING THE JESUS SEED

Damon was a nice guy and his friends welcomed me into their group. I enjoyed the more relaxed party feel of that rental house, and I was more myself in an atmosphere that felt like what I'd enjoyed with my Bennington bar buddies.

During one of Damon's house parties, I met a sweet young Hungarian girl named Agnes. In Hungarian her name means "chaste" and she certainly was. She was a Christian with an innocent loving nature who didn't do drugs and barely drank alcohol.

She showed me the unconditional acceptance that my wounded spirit longed for and showered me with the attention that my childhood self believed was how love was supposed to look. It was the perfect opportunity for me to heal my broken self, get an unlimited flow of what I thought was love, and slowly mend my self-love into one that allowed me to genuinely care for myself and love others. The influence of her Christianity also helped water the Jesus seed in my heart.

Agnes gave me her undivided attention, never judged my actions, and chose me to have sex with for her first time. She came into my life to show me unconditional love, but I was too wounded to recognize the gift I'd been given. While all she wanted to do was give of herself, all my hurting self wanted to do was take. Jesus had sent someone to help heal my heart and water His seed, but as the novelty of the relationship wore off, all I saw was someone who didn't share my love of drugs.

After about six months of dating Agnes, Damon found out the house we rented was being sold and we had to find another place to rent. I found an apartment in Aurora, an eastern suburb of Denver. Agnes and I continued to date on and off until the City of Aurora decided they wanted me to live in their detention center.

12 LIFE IN A DUMPSTER

One Friday night I was driving around Aurora, Colorado in my Honda Civic and stopped at a gas station for gas and cigarettes. I spotted a police squad car when I went inside to buy cigarettes but didn't think much of it.

As I walked back to my car one of the officers approached me. "May I see your license sir?" the officer asked. "I'm old enough to buy cigarettes," I joked. "Your license, sir?" I handed over my license. The officer looked at it for a moment and announced, "Travis, Morse, you're under arrest."

Of all the things I had done in my life, partying, drugs, sex, working, sleeping, and eating, one thing I never made time to do was to go to court for traffic violations. Previously when I was pulled over and charged with possession of marijuana in Denver I was given a date to appear in court. Another time when I was pulled over for speeding in Aurora I was also given a date to appear in court. When the court dates came and went without me appearing before a judge, warrants were issued for my arrest. These arrest warrants meant a police officer could immediately throw me in jail to sit and wait to appear before a judge for those violations.

That's exactly what that officer did. He brought me to Aurora County Detention Center where I was fingerprinted and processed. Courts aren't open on weekends so I had to sit in the detention center until Monday morning. That's the bad news. The good news is that for breakfast, Aurora County Detention Center served Fruity Pebbles cereal! It was a bright spot in my otherwise dismal existence in the detention center. Once I went before a judge for the Aurora speeding ticket, they transferred me to Denver to go before a judge there for the marijuana possession charge.

Big city courts have a backlog of cases. I sat in

Denver County Jail for a few weeks until a judge could see me. During those weeks I got sober, ate well, and read the Bible the jail provided. Finally, my court date arrived. While I was negotiating to get probation for the misdemeanor marijuana possession charge, my landlord was relocating all of my apartment belongings into his parking lot's dumpster.

After my release from Denver County jail, I took public transportation back to the gas station to get my car. The policemen told me it was fine to leave my car there during my stay in the detention center. He didn't know I'd be transferred to another jail for a few weeks. When I got to the gas station, my car had been towed. I paid the ransom for it and drove to my apartment to find some of my belongings laying in, or next to the dumpster. Scavengers had rummaged through them before I arrived.

Most of my things were replaceable except for two sentimental items – a photo book my mom had made for me about my childhood and my treasured Bible from Toby Mac. I climbed into the dumpster to search for both of those and didn't find either. I was so devastated I sat down in the garbage and cried. My apartment was gone. My two important possessions were gone. Agnes was gone. Sitting in that filth I noticed some of my liquor buried beneath the trash. I opened up the bottle of Sailor Jerry and sat there for the next hour, soaking my brain with 80-proof spiced rum.

13 METH GIRL

After the eviction from the Aurora apartment, a coworker named Marcie generously let me sleep on her couch for a while.

One Friday night while I was still at Marcie's, I got a call from a guy, Donnie, a fellow inmate from Marble Valley Correctional Center. He was visiting Colorado and I suggested we meet up somewhere in the city. We decided on a small, seedy strip club north of Denver.

The liquor flowed, the girls were friendly, and Donnie and I had a great time. When the place was ready to close, Donnie headed out. Some of the strippers asked me if I'd like to continue the party at a local motel. Both of my heads thought their invitation was going to be something mind-blowing.

I rented a motel room and we smoked weed and did endless lines of cocaine. The girls danced around and it became obvious all they wanted to do was tease and get high. I felt like an outsider to their clique. Fortunately, a group who were partying next door heard our party and asked to join us. One of them was a heavenly young redhead with enchanting hazel eyes named Becky. We became fast friends.

By sunrise the strippers disbanded and Becky's friends left to get breakfast. She stayed back in my room to be with me. Sober thinking would have made both of us question what might be beginning between us. With both of us still high, she didn't hesitate to cozy up to a stranger who had just spent a cocaine-fueled all-nighter in a cheap motel with strippers. I willingly overlooked that she wasn't the least bit apprehensive about being alone with someone like me.

Once everyone left we made small talk, did a few lines of coke, and quickly ended up in bed. It was a wonderful release after all the teasing I had endured the night before. To cloud my judgment even more, my orgasm added the brain chemicals dopamine and oxytocin on top of my high. I quickly fell in love with her and we spent the next few days in my room getting high and having sex.

Meeting her changed my life. I'd finally found another girl who delivered my childhood version of love and attention, plus she liked to do drugs. My hardened heart softened and tricked me into thinking I'd found true love. My neediness made me jump in with both feet. I couldn't get enough of her and wanted to build my life around this girl.

Hanging out with her presented some challenges. I couldn't bring her to Marcie's house and we couldn't party at her place because she lived with her parents. To hook up we had to keep renting motel rooms. Between paying for motels and drugs, my paychecks weren't lasting until the next one. I needed more money.

Next to Rent-A-Center was a liquor store. The owner of that liquor store had previously approached me and promised a much higher paycheck. Chasing more money, I quit Rent-A-Center and went to work for the liquor store. Had I possessed a clear head, I might have recognized that taking that job wasn't the best long-term career choice for me. Instead, I jumped at the job and quickly realized I'd made a mistake. The owner's culture and language differences made our working relationship difficult. I dreaded coming to work and made another impulsive decision to quit, certain I could return to Rent-A-Center. But when I approached my old boss, he had to follow corporate hiring procedures which included a background check which he didn't do when I transferred to the Denver location from Vermont. This check showed some driving problems on my record that eliminated me from being considered for employment. I was out of work again.

Becky helped me find a new job near where she lived. She had a friend, Brad, who managed a pizza place in her neighborhood. He hired me to work there as an assistant manager. Because Becky and my job were in the south suburbs, I decided my apartment should be also. I got an apartment within walking distance of the pizza place.

The pizza place was a source of income, but I needed

something more substantial. After a short time at the pizza place, Becky got her friend at an electronic warehouse to help me get a new job as their inventory and receiving manager. There I made a new coworker friend, Martell. In the future, he'd be the guy who let me put my camper next to his garage when I had to move it off of Sean's property.

Becky's interest in being with me and the love hormones that soaked my brain tricked me into thinking I was lovable. My internal pain lessened and the negative self-talk subsided. Being around Becky made me feel wonderful. I'd found a soul mate who enjoyed my favorite activities -- sex and drugs. Life was great.

My love-drunk mind ignored so many warning signs and kept me from asking probing questions about her life. If I had, I would have learned that the recreational drugs we did were minor league compared to what she'd done before I met her. When we started dating she was on a self-imposed hiatus from smoking methamphetamines and was only able to keep away from them because the newness of our relationship distracted her mind.

Neither of us had lost our demons. They were just

being placated by a steady diet of weed, coke, dopamine, and oxytocin.

14 BROKEN PEOPLE

When drug abusers first enter recovery, their long-term goal isn't to stop their physical dependency as much as to try to eradicate the psychological triggers driving their addiction. That is why a good portion of the recovery process is spent baring their souls, finally telling the truth, and letting their emotions express themselves. The hope is during these confessions the addicts can identify their demons and what they're feeding on. The next step is reframing or correcting the views of the traumas that created them. Until that's accomplished, the addiction will continue to wreak havoc on their lives.

Placating the demons to quiet them doesn't make them go away. Because of this, rehab programs discourage people in recovery from starting relationships with each other. In recovery meetings, addicts drop their guard and allow themselves to be vulnerable. This honesty and vulnerability can be attractive to other group members who have lived their lives filled with fear and lies.

Relationships between group members seem natural and these people in the group might be good partners if they'd met under normal circumstances. The risk of these relationships, however, and the reason they are discouraged within the first year of sobriety, is because the brain chemicals associated with new love provide a replacement euphoria. The addict thinks they've lost their desire for drugs when they've substituted one brain chemical for another.

The danger of replacing illegal drugs with these love hormones is that once the relationship settles into a comfortable routine, the euphoria subsides. If the relationship ends, the pain of the breakup can cause their demons to grow even stronger. This was the course my relationship with Becky was taking.

While I was still crazy about her, Becky showed signs

she considered our relationship routine and was slowly pulling away. She began using meth again. I sensed a difference in her, but I ignored it. Eventually, she told me about her past use and how her interest in the drug returned. I was okay with her using meth as long as she stayed my girlfriend.

Becky downplayed the frequency of her meth use and acted distressed that she was smoking it again. I told her if she wanted to stop it completely I'd support her. She said, "It's not that easy, Travis. It's irresistible." I thought about all the cocaine I had done in the past and how I walked away from it without a problem. I questioned her resolve. She insisted meth was this incredibly magnetic drug.

To prove my point that any drug was resistible, I agreed to try some meth. One Saturday night she came over to my apartment and pulled out a glass pipe from her purse. It was different from any pipe I'd seen used for smoking weed. There was a bubble at the end with a hole in the top where she dropped in the methamphetamine crystals. Then she took a lighter and began the process of melting it. She showed me how she warmed the melted meth while she rocked the pipe side to side and inhaled. It stunk like ammonia or cat urine. Soon she handed it to me.

She worked the lighter while I sucked on the glass tube. As the meth vapors reached my mouth they burned my lips, gums, and tongue. There was nothing pleasurable about meth compared to my beloved weed. Much like the first time you drink a beer and wince at the bitterness, or take your first drag of a cigarette and cough and choke, if I was ever going to like meth I'd have to ignore the distasteful smell and burning effects to acquire a taste for the high. The thought of doing that was unappealing because the high was overshadowed by the drug sickness I felt from poisoning my body with meth.

For three days I hung out with Becky and her friends and smoked it. I felt like crap. The effects of the amphetamine were like drinking a case of Red Bull. I was grinding my teeth, had cottonmouth, was jittery, easily agitated, and wanted to jump out of my itchy skin. The high didn't let me sleep, and once the high disappeared I felt immediately exhausted. That sucked too, so I smoked more to get back my energy. We partied and had sex that lasted for hours. By Tuesday night she ran out of meth. Exhausted, I said, "Enough!" I crashed in my apartment and slept for a day. When I woke I realized I'd missed several days of work. Again, I'd succeeded in sabotaging myself.

15 BEGINNING OF THE END

Fortunately, I kept my warehouse job telling them I had the flu and couldn't do anything but sleep. They gave me a second chance, but told me if I did that again I was fired. I didn't see that as a problem because meth wasn't magnetic. It was annoying! I was happy sticking to my weed, dopamine, and oxytocin to get my highs. I wasn't going to judge my girlfriend if she used it because her drug-abusing behavior still fit well within the low standards I expected for my friends.

Becky fell back into her meth addiction and wanted

to be around her addicted crowd. She came up with more and more excuses not to see me. "My parents want me home." "I'm not feeling well." "We'll get together this weekend. I promise!" I believed her excuses because the alternative would be I'd have to admit the self-esteem-crushing reality that doing meth and being with her drug friends meant more to her than being with me.

Seeing Becky less, I got stoned more to silence my sadness and the gnawing questions I had about her. Becky's excuses increased until I reached a point where I had to admit that meth was Becky's new lover. I also suspected that her lack of interest in sex with me meant she was getting it from someone within her drug group. I needed to face reality.

One day in February I was working at the warehouse and tried for the umpteenth time to reach Becky on her phone. She was ignoring me and I'd had enough. I was going to track her down during my lunch break and confront her. I knew the friend's house she frequented when she partied, and I suspected she could be found there.

I punched out of work and got in my Civic. Blinded by rage and a midday winter storm I headed out to find her. I blasted my radio to match the level of the shouting in my head as I drove well above the speed limit through the blizzard.

My wipers did a poor job of keeping my windshield clear and I noticed too late I was approaching an intersection where the traffic light was transitioning from yellow to red. I hit the brakes, certain I could stop in time. I hadn't factored in black ice, and my car slid into two of the eighteen wheels of a passing tractor-trailer. The airbag hesitated, allowing me to lunge forward through the windshield and onto my hood. I jumped off the hood filled with adrenaline and shock. I told the truck driver I was fine and then I collapsed.

Paramedics brought me to the hospital for observation. I had cuts on my head, a broken collar bone, and a damaged knee. Becky's friend at the warehouse told her what happened and she rushed to the hospital.

Lying in the hospital bed, my anger seethed, knowing my car was damaged on top of my relationship with Becky. When she walked in the door I immediately accused her of being a meth addict and cheating on me. She admitted both and I shouted, "GET OUT!"

She welcomed her release from our relationship. Later that same day I got a visit from a Jefferson County Sheriff. "Travis Morse?" I lifted my hand as if to say, "Here." He handed me some papers and said, "You're being charged with reckless driving." I was requested to appear in Jefferson County Court for an arraignment hearing in two months.

That court appearance would be another one I'd miss, adding to the ongoing list of warrants for my arrest, and a continuation of my long relationship with Colorado law enforcement, courts, and jails.

16 TWO STEPS BACK

Though I wasn't using it, meth succeeded in screwing up my life. The accident with the truck totaled my car and I didn't have collision insurance or the money to get it fixed. Without transportation to my job, I got fired.

Three months after the accident I was in my apartment enjoying a breakfast joint when there was a sharp knocking on my door. I heard a muffled announcement, "Jefferson County Sheriff!"

Did Becky rat me out?! I grabbed anything that looked

like drug paraphernalia and shoved it in my bottom dresser drawer beneath my underwear. *Should I flush the weed down the toilet? It's good weed and cost me a lot!* The second thumping on the door was more impatient and I shouted, "I'm coming!" I threw the weed in the drawer, grabbed a clean shirt, sprayed the living room with an air freshener, and headed to face my fate. Out of breath and sweating, I opened the door. There stood two officers from the Jefferson County Sheriff's department.

"Travis Morse? May we see your license?" the tall one asked. "Yes, what's going on?" The short one compared the information on my license to a list they'd brought along. *Was this legal? Wasn't there something called probable cause? Should I ask if they have a warrant?* They scanned the information and it turned out they had a warrant for my arrest. It was for failure to appear a month earlier on my court date for the car accident. *Well, at least it wasn't for the possession of marijuana!*

I'd been so preoccupied with getting stoned to forget about the pain of my bruised collar bone, dislocated knee, the mess of not having a car or job or rent money, or Becky that I'd forgotten to attend my accident arraignment hearing.

They handcuffed me and escorted me to their vehicle. It looked like Colorado law enforcement wasn't going to be as relaxed as in Bennington.

For the next two weeks, I waited in Jefferson County jail for my arraignment hearing. It was horrible. I had plenty of time to relive every aspect of my relationship with Becky and to speculate on ways I could have avoided the ending. I beat myself up for being so foolish as to open my heart so she could stomp all over it. And, I had to admit, she succeeded in tricking me into thinking anyone would ever love me. What was worse about those two weeks of soul-searching is I didn't have weed to numb the pain of my crumbling self-esteem.

On arraignment day the judge convicted me of reckless driving. It held a possible sentence of weeks in jail and a couple of hundred dollars in fines. I pleaded with the judge telling him about the black ice and asking him not to give me more jail time. He sentenced me to time served and to pay a fine of $1000. My driver's license was tagged with four demerit points. Six more and I'd get my driver's license revoked. I had some money, but not $1,000. Tyler lent me some and I pawned a few of my possessions to get the rest. The week after I got out of jail I was evicted from my apartment. I moved in with my brother's fiancé Sara. She lived a mile from my apartment. I went back to the pizza place to resume my management job and to continue the ride on my rollercoaster life.

17 TRY, TRY AGAIN

Tyler's life with Sara was moving forward while mine kept taking steps back. Sara spent more and more time at my brother's place, leaving me to have the apartment to myself. I enjoyed a free place to stay and a familiar job back at the pizza place.

Tyler's roommate moved out and Sara moved in. Soon they would marry and start a family. Tyler offered to let me live up north with them temporarily. His house was near a bowling alley and I easily landed a job there working the front counter.

The bowling alley job was uplifting. People came there to have fun. I watched couples and groups and families have great times. During slow periods I'd practice, and eventually I joined their bowling league. I even put together a team from regulars I'd watched who played well. Our team did very well and I thrived on the weekly camaraderie and competition.

One of my teammates, Roger, told me his daughter was moving to Denver from Minnesota. She and her husband were separating and she was moving back in with Roger and his wife. A few weeks later a short, attractive brunette came to sit with us while our team was playing. Roger introduced her as his daughter Erika, and she became our one-woman cheering section. I played a little better that night.

Erika became a weekly regular and I could feel chemistry developing between us. She started coming to the bowling alley on days when her dad wasn't playing. I could see where our friendship was going and I told my brother I needed to move out. I was making decent money and found a room for rent on Craig's List. The owner of the house was an electrician named Angelo. He rented the room to me for $500 a month. I also bought a Ford Ranger with only fifty-thousands miles. After four years in Colorado, my life was looking up again.

When Erika wasn't over at my place, we hung out at

a bar called Bad Dog Bar & Grill. We enjoyed the energy of that lively, noisy place with a country music soundtrack. She was fun to be with and I drank very little during our dating. Weed, oxytocin, and dopamine provided all the highs I needed.

After a few months of dating, we decided to get our own place. We found a duplex to rent for $800 a month. Tyler saw how serious I was getting with Erika, and he found me a good service position in the heating and air conditioning business where he worked. I built control panels, managed their warehouse, and drove their service vehicles to a shop for repairs.

Whenever I drove their service vehicles I'd put gas in them. I was given a company credit card. I didn't understand corporate accounting and the importance of separating company and personal expenses. If I took a company vehicle to get fuel, I'd charge a couple of packs of cigarettes, snacks, and a drink.

I did this for a while until the company accountant noticed the charges on my receipts and brought it to the attention of my boss. He fired me on the spot for using corporate funds to buy personal items. My brother was disappointed and embarrassed, but not surprised. His little brother had screwed up again.

I felt like an idiot, but I wasn't going to let this mistake cause me to lose my duplex because I couldn't pay for rent. I contacted my previous landlord, Angelo, and he found me an opportunity as a journeyman electrician where he worked. The pay was good and the work was interesting. I was back on track.

Erika and I were making a life together. My paycheck covered our expenses and Erika contributed her monthly government disability check she received because of her Muscular Dystrophy (M.S.). We didn't talk about marriage, but eventually, we filed joint income taxes, which in the eyes of the state meant we were claiming to be a common-law couple. It was as binding as being married without all the legal paperwork or ceremony.

I built my skills as an electrician while Erika stayed at home. We got a rescue dog from Dumb Friends League and named him Bailey, after Champ Bailey of the Denver Broncos. I had a nice place to live, a good woman, and a dog. We only needed one more piece to make us a family.

18 A RAY OF HOPE

One of the only goals I've ever had for my life was to have a child by the time I was thirty years old. I can't explain exactly why I set that timeline. All I know is it came from something deep inside me.

Maybe I wanted to see if I could succeed where my father had failed. Or possibly I wanted to create someone I could love without fear or reservation, knowing their history from the beginning. Someone who didn't bring baggage into the relationship. Someone I could trust to love me without fear of them ending our relationship later when their truths surfaced and their traumas damaged our love.

Creating a child would put me permanently in a

father-child relationship. That relationship could never truly end. I knew this because even though my father was not in my life, his connection to me as my father is why the hurt from his desertion continued to haunt my soul and damage my life. I promised myself when I had a child it would be different.

I worked hard at my electrician job so I could provide a great life for Erika and eventually a comfortable life for our family. We were excited when Erika discovered she was pregnant. It seemed like a natural next step for us and I was happy I'd be reaching my parenting goal.

The months flew by until we were getting closer to the baby's birth date. Erika had Braxton-Hicks contractions known as false indications of labor. We didn't know the difference so we rushed to the hospital. I dropped her off while I found a place to park. Our mistake turned out to be a blessing because there was something with her M.S. that made delivering a baby extremely quickly! By the time I parked the car and got to Erika, our baby was already exiting her womb. Very soon we had a new six-pound four-ounce son. Tanner Jordan Morse.

I was overwhelmed by the love I felt for this child.

My eyes teared up when I saw how little and helpless he was. I held him in my arms and whispered to him, "I promise to be the best father to you."

We brought him home a few days later and got him settled into his new room. Erika took to motherhood easily. It was wonderful to watch Tanner grow and develop. We were excited when he slept through the night, walked his first steps, and learned to live without diapers.

I felt like I was at the top of my game but in reality, I was at the top of a rollercoaster.

19 MORE STEPS BACK

Life was going well. I had a loving wife, a young son, a dog, and a rented duplex that was feeling more and more like a real home. My life had stabilized and settled into a routine.

I started and ended each day by taking Champ outside by the patio for a pee and poop while I enjoyed a cigarette. I didn't smoke inside our home. As much as I liked cigarettes, I didn't want to be in places that smelled like them. So, anytime I needed a cigarette I smoked them outside my home, outside my car, and outside my work.

At our rental there was a swamp cooler outside next

to our patio; much like how air conditioning units sit next to houses. It had a metal drip pan underneath it that became my ashtray. Anytime I smoked outside, that tray was where my cigarette butts ended up.

One snowy evening in January I came home from work, ate dinner, watched TV with the family, and had a cigarette on the patio before I went to bed. At about 3 AM we woke to a pungent smell. Bailey was on the bed and I thought he might have farted. Looking in the hallway I noticed an orange glow. I went to investigate and saw flames outside my kitchen window just as the window exploded inward. The fire climbed through the window and the glass shards on the kitchen floor glistened orange from the blaze. I ran back into our bedroom and shook Erika to wake her as I yelled, "Fire!". Her M.S. made her move slowly, so I grabbed some clothes for her, yanked my son out of his crib, scooped up Bailey in my other arm and we headed out the door with only a minute to spare.

We stood across the street improperly dressed for the weather and watched the quickly spreading inferno burn our dreams to the ground. A neighbor let me call Tyler and he picked us up and took us to his home.

Later that morning we drove back to look at the damage. Fortunately, the connected house was saved from burning thanks to the quick action of the first responders and the firewall that separated our rental from the other side of the duplex. Unfortunately, our side was burned to the ground and we didn't have renters insurance.

We stayed at my brother's house for a few days, then moved in with Erika's parents. A few months later we found a basement for rent in Golden. We were like nomads moving from place to place, but at least I still had a steady job. That is until the owner of the electrical place where I worked died and his son took over the business. This kid had no business or people sense and proceeded to drive the business into the ground. I quit, refusing to work for such incompetence.

Things looked a little better when we left the basement rental and found a two-bedroom house to rent in Golden. I also landed a job at a nuclear filter technology company working on their assembly line.

It looked like our life had turned a corner. I was back in a house with my wife, son, and dog and I was working at a good job. We purchased some secondhand furniture and slowly put our lives back together. I had everything I needed and wasn't going to do anything to sabotage it. Instead, Erika would take a turn.

20 DOWNWARD SPIRAL

Life was looking up. We all survived the fire unscathed and had family in the area to help us out until we got back on our feet. Tyler and Sara had their second son, Blake. We lived close by and visited them often. Blake and his older brother, Reece became close buddies with Tanner.

I had a new job I liked and Erika was a good mom to baby Tanner. While he played with his toys on the floor, she played with her computer on the Internet.

I went to work and Erika took care of our home. We

settled into a comfortable routine. Life went smoothly for a while until I noticed a growing indifference in Erika's attitude toward me. She criticized me more and we argued over little things. I sensed something was bothering her and I asked her about it. She denied anything had changed on her end of the relationship, but eventually during a heated argument she admitted she'd met someone online. Her admission pulled the rug out from under me. I was speechless as she told me she thought we should separate.

I had a comfortable life and didn't want it to change. I dutifully went to work every day and brought home a good paycheck that supported the family and kept me supplied with weed. I came home on time the majority of evenings except when I visited with my weed dealer to replenish my supply. Once I settled in for the evening, I'd smoke up and watch sports while I waited for Erika to make my dinner. I ate in front of the TV while she put Tanner to bed.

Within two months, that idyllic life changed drastically. Erika kept Tanner and went to stay with her parents. I kept the house and spent most nights wallowing with my buddies at the Bad Dog Bar & Grill.

Then the filter company I worked for merged with another and there was a mass layoff. I was one of the casualties. Bad Dog needed a cook so I took the job. Without Erika's income, and my making less money, I had to find a way to supplement the rent. One of my friends at the bar, Phil, installed hardwood flooring and asked me to help him with his jobs. I mentioned to Phil that I could no longer afford the rent on my own. He offered to let me live in a shed on his land. I left the rental house and moved into his place. That's when I learned he was also a crop farmer. His crop? Marijuana! Maybe my luck had turned around! I was living in his shed rent-free and had an endless supply of weed right outside my door! No longer did I have to go trolling the seedy parts of the city to score some dope.

I stayed in Phil's shed and helped him with flooring jobs. I also worked for extra cash at the Bad Dog, and in a bar nearby called Outlook Tavern as a bar back.

Things went well for about six months until Phil told me he needed to sell his property and move away. Dave, the owner of the Outlook Tavern leased a repair garage next to his bar where he said I could stay. It had a bathroom, shower, and place for me to set up a bed. The Outlook became my work and social life.

I had no joy in my life except for the times I'd get a weekend with my son Tanner. We did sleepovers in Phil's shed and Dave's garage. He didn't care where I lived. He just liked being around his dad. I left the garage and rented an apartment across the street from the Outlook Tavern. Erika was much happier seeing Tanner stay in a real apartment when she dropped him off on weekends. Though we were separated, she always wanted the best for me and knew how much I loved my son. Erika did her best to let me see Tanner whenever I wanted.

After two months of living in that apartment, I started to itch. I soon discovered the entire apartment was infested with bed bugs. I had to throw out all of my belongings. It was like having another fire without the flames. I moved back into the garage.

Then one Friday I was driving my Ford pickup to Outlook Tavern for an evening of partying away my money and didn't notice my speed. I got pulled over by a Colorado Sheriff. He ran my license and found I had another outstanding arrest warrant. I'd had a minor traffic ticket that my stoner mind completely erased from my memory. When I didn't pay it, Colorado issued a warrant for my arrest.

The officer handcuffed me and brought me directly to Adams County Sheriff's Detention Facility. It was a tan, two-story bunker-looking concrete building with vertical slits for windows surrounded by tall fences topped with barbed wire. I wanted to be hanging around with my bar buddies, but instead, I was being strip-searched, fingerprinted, posing for a mugshot, and being sent to a holding tank dressed in a black and white striped outfit. When the processing was completed, I was given a set of bright yellow scrubs to wear among the other inmates, referred to as the "population." I couldn't go before a judge until Monday.

On Monday I saw the judge and paid for the ticket. They dragged their feet on processing my release and I didn't walk out of there until Tuesday at 2 AM. The detention facility was in Brighton, twenty-three miles from the automobile garage. I had no transportation because the Sheriff had towed and impounded my truck. I was pissed. For the next five hours, I walked through all kinds of neighborhoods until I made it back to the garage.

I got my truck out of the impound and sold it to get more money. Then I bought a cheap little red car just to get around. It wasn't long before I was pulled over for another traffic violation, ignored the court date, and was taken to another detention center on an arrest warrant. This time I left my little car in the impound. I just didn't care.

My life felt like it was on a slippery slope. I couldn't find a decent place to live and I no longer spent my days with my wife, son, and dog. I was barely making enough money to support my nomad lifestyle.

I spent most of my money trying to silence the mocking voice of my battered self-esteem telling me I couldn't keep a good woman and that I didn't deserve to have my son in my life full-time. I was getting exactly what my unlovable, unworthy self deserved. To mute the voice I tried smoking lots of weed, snorting cocaine, and drinking never enough alcohol. I felt like I was sleeping walking through a nightmare. I didn't think my life could get worse. My demons assured me this was just the beginning.

21 THE DEVIL INCARNATE

My days at Outlook Tavern blended from one to the next. Each consisted of hours of mind-numbing chatter with the same regulars repeating the same tired comments while we lubricated ourselves with the same intoxicating substances. Then she walked in.

I was behind the bar stocking the liquor bottles when an unfamiliar young woman walked up and asked for a beer. "Do you have a particular one in mind?" I asked. "Whatever's cheapest," she replied. I looked into her deep blue eyes as I handed her a can of

Pabst Blue Ribbon and said, "It's on the house."

She walked over to a pool table to knock some balls around. Most of my buddies' eyes were on her as she bent over the pool table to coax balls into the pockets. Her style was amateurish, but her form was excellent. I walked over to the table to offer we play a game.

"Hi, I'm Travis."
"Valerie," she said as she concentrated on her next shot rather than me.
"Can I play with you?" I asked, meaning it in every sense of the word.
"Sure," she said, holding up her empty beer can, "As long as you keep buyin'."

We played a little pool and drank a lot. When we were both sufficiently numb, I suggested we go to my place in the garage. Together we stumbled to the building next door. The sex was sloppy but felt great after a considerable dry spell.

This scenario repeated itself over the next few days. Eventually, I suggested we go to her place instead. I figured it had to be better than mine. It wasn't. She was squatting in a shed behind another bar; much like the small shed I lived in on Phil's property. Her place had a sleeping bag on the floor, a chair, a small table, and a plastic storage container where she kept her clothes. The condition of her place didn't matter to me. As long as I ended up with her in the sleeping bag, I was happy. While she was straightening up her place to make it a little more presentable to a guy who didn't care one way or the other, I pulled out a joint and started smoking it. She took a few tokes off it and said, "If you want to smoke, I've got something even better!" She reached into a bag on the floor and pulled out a glass pipe like Becky's. Then reached into a large bucket to pick out some crystals.

I'd seen crystals of meth before but never in this quantity. She had what seemed like an endless supply of the stuff. She lit the pipe and shared it with me. The smell and burning sensation were less annoying that time and the high was better. After we smoked a few of the crystals we spent the rest of the night and most of the morning in that sleeping bag. I couldn't tell if the exhaustion I felt was from all the sex or the meth leaving my system, but whatever the cause, doing another bubble gave me energy again.

Being with Valerie and smoking meth was exciting

and different from the humdrum of my usual life at Outlook Tavern. She moved into the garage with me. Each new day we spent high on oxytocin and dopamine from the sex, and the major shots of dopamine the meth released into our systems, on top of the orgasms. Life was grand!

Valerie introduced me to her meth dealer, an upper-middle-class businessman who supplemented his legitimate business by trafficking methamphetamine. From the day I met him I never understood why he dealt illegal drugs when his primary legitimate business was successful. He was generous with his meth, seeming more interested in distributing it than making money from it. We didn't care. Thanks to him we had an endless supply of the stuff for little or no cost.

Shortly after I met Valerie, Dave, the Outlook Tavern owner died from rapidly progressing pancreatic cancer. His decline was quick and ugly. His best friend took over the lease to keep the bar open, but the owner of the building did an inspection of the property to complete the transaction and saw that someone was living in the garage. He told Dave's friend the garage was not zoned for residential and we had to leave. Next stop – Hell.

22 LIFE IN THE TOILET

Valerie had succeeded where Becky failed. I was hooked on methamphetamines. Before we got kicked out of the automobile garage Valerie and I enjoyed an endless supply of meth and sex. The time we spent at Outlook Tavern decreased, but my income didn't because I took up a profitable new hobby – shoplifting. Stealing from stores was a rush when high because meth gave me an inflated sense of confidence and boldness, plus the Bronco sportswear I stole was easy to sell to the bar crowd.

Soon I became friends with Valerie's dealer. He was

paranoid that the DEA was onto his operations and he gave me meth in buckets just to offload his supply. Just like Becky, meth became my new lover. The dopamine release I experienced from sex was no match for the megadoses released when smoking meth. Valerie's friendship was no longer a priority. I had a cheap, endless supply of dopamine-releasing meth and that was fine with me. The problem with not hanging out with Valerie anymore is that I'd need somewhere else to smoke meth. I no longer lived in the garage and couldn't afford to rent.

One day after leaving the dealer with a bucket of meth, I walked around the city looking for a place to use my new stash. With a bucket of meth, you can make friends quickly on the streets. As I walked, I noticed some street people that I could tell were fellow meth users, commonly called "tweakers." I opened up my bucket and we got high together. I left them with some crystals and continued on my way. As I continued my walk, I saw homeless people who looked like they had no income. I gave them a few crystals to sell to make cash. I wandered around high and aimless for a while until the sun was dropping, and so was my energy. I needed to find another place that wasn't Valerie's shed to do another bubble. I found a handicapped portable toilet at a secluded public park near Outlook Tavern. I smoked my bubble there. It became my place to hang out and crash overnight if I needed to sleep. When it came time to clean up, I visited convenience stores, grabbed handfuls of napkins, and headed to their bathroom. When I needed fresh clothes I used a laundromat or stole new ones. During the day I'd stop in Outlook Tavern to socialize with my bar buddies. I'd make a few dollars stocking the bar or selling sports gear. More often than not, Valerie was one of the regulars and if I needed sex, she was always willing.

I stayed in that toilet for about a month before one of the regulars at Outlook Tavern learned where I was staying and offered an old camper he had on the back of an unused pickup truck on his property. I was excited about the idea because during the month I'd been living in the toilet I'd been holding off having my son visit. Living in a camper meant his mother would let him visit with me again. I was excited about seeing him and teaching him my new hobby.

23 MOVIN' ON UP

Living in the camper was an upgrade and getting to see my son on weekends was so nice. Tanner lived with his mom and his grandparents during the week. Then on the weekends, he'd come to visit me. For my six-year-old, living in a camper out in an open field made it seem like we were camping.

When Sean had to sell his property and move the camper, my old coworker Martell was kind enough to let me situate the camper on a concrete pad next to his garage. He made me a key for his house so that when I needed a bathroom I could go inside his home. That bathroom came in handy when my son was visiting. He could use it instead of peeing in a field and I could use it to smoke a quick bubble whenever my high started to fade.

I tried to make Tanner's visits to the camper more fun. I took him to a pet shop where we bought a cage and some pet ducks. We had the cage outside under the sleeper area of the camper. That was fun for a while until a wild animal visited one night and made the ducks its dinner. The next pet I got him was Mr. Thumper, a lion-headed rabbit. It was good-natured and the long fur around its face made him look like he had a lion's mane. Tanner and I put Mr. Thumper on a leash and took walks to the nearby park. I can't imagine what the neighbors thought about the crazy white guy from the rubber-coated camper who walked a lion-looking rabbit on a leash with his son down Martin Luther King Jr. Boulevard. I didn't think much about it because I was enjoying time with my son, and usually high as a kite.

One night a wild animal visited Mr. Thumper in his cage and that was the end of that pet. I bought Tanner another rabbit, but this time I kept it inside the camper in a cabinet. I didn't want his new pet to lose its life while living with me at the camper.

Another fun activity I enjoyed with my young son while floating high in methland was painting a bicycle as a tribute to my beloved Broncos. I got some orange and blue spray paint for the tires and I painted the rest of the bike with the black rubber paint I had from painting the camper. The idea in my head of the Bronco bike sounded cool, but painting it with a methed-up mind, the execution became a disaster. By the time I finished with the black rubber paint on the wheels, gears, and chain the bike became an inoperable mess. It got added to the rest of the trash that was collecting on the outside of my camper.

One day I got the brilliant idea to take my son on an adventure. We'd ride the light rail train to my favorite department store to steal some Bronco jerseys. My son was excited to ride the train, having no clue about the dumb idea I had in mind for him when we got to the store. I was high on meth while I put one Bronco jersey after another onto my son's small frame. Meth emboldened me and made me oblivious to reality. My criminal activity was obvious to everyone including store security.

The police were called and the officer was nice enough to let me and my son go, but not until he got enough information to file a Reckless Endangerment against me. Child Services got involved and the courts decided I should not see my son anymore. My life on meth was crashing down, and it was about to burn.

24 BAPTISM BY FIRE

I was tired of living my rollercoaster life. I no longer had my son visiting, but I did have his rabbit to keep me company. Unfortunately, every time I looked at it I was reminded Tanner wasn't coming around anymore.

I fell into a deep depression and for a month I used more and more meth to combat it. I did so much meth I barely slept at all. One chilly night toward the end of the month I sat at the small table with the warmth of the space heater on my legs. I called my mother to share my sorrows. I sat petting Tanner's rabbit on my lap and I told her about how not being able to see my son was more than I could bear. Without my son in my life, I just wanted to die. She reassured me life would get better. I doubted she was right.

After we talked, I turned on the TV and watched hours of mindless programs while I sat there wishing my life would end. I grabbed my Bible on the chance some verse could give me hope. I opened to Proverbs chapter 5 and noticed verses 21 to 23:

> *For your ways are in full view of the Lord, and he examines all your paths. The evil deed of the wicked ensnare them; the cords of their sins hold them fast. For lack of discipline, they will die, led astray by their own great folly.*

Was God trying to tell me He was watching while I self-destructed? I turned to my other favorite book, Psalms, and read the beginning of chapter 6.

> *Lord, do not rebuke me in your anger or discipline me in your wrath. Have mercy on me, Lord, for I am faint; heal me, Lord, for my bones are in agony. My soul is in deep anguish. How long, Lord, how long?*

Yes, how long did I have to live like this? The

thought that my life was going to continue this way weighed on my mind. Exhausted from the depression and lack of sleep, I put Tanner's rabbit back in its cabinet and climbed up into my bed.

I must have fallen asleep because at some point I was startled awake by a burning sensation on my leg. I woke to find the bottom of my covers on fire and the whole trailer engulfed in flames. The smell of burning flesh and the toxic fumes of the melting rubber walls filled my nose. I was trapped in the small sleeping compartment on the opposite side of the camper's door. The smoke from the burning rubber made it difficult to see or breathe. *I'm going to die! I wanted my screwed-up life to end and God is granting me my wish! But this isn't the way I wanted it to end! Jesus, get me out of here! If you save me I promise I will turn my life around!*

With little room to move and my bedding on fire, I desperately kicked at the corner until the riveted seam gave way. I rolled on my belly and pushed myself out of the camper and tumbled onto the ground just as the top of the camper blew off in a fiery explosion.

I crawled away to safety in disbelief, watching as my life and Martell's garage went up in flames.

PART THREE

25 SON OF MAN

In the Bible's book of Matthew, Chapter 18, Verse 11, it is written, *"For the Son of Man has come to save that which was lost."*

Throughout my journey to find love and numb the pain of my father's rejection, I wandered around from one empty relationship to another. Not knowing what true love looked like I pursued a childish idea of what it was. Compounding my efforts were all the drugs I took to dull the voice of unworthiness playing in my head. From the outside it appeared I was never going to experience real love. Looking back, however, I can see true love was with me all along.

When I invited Jesus into my life at fifteen, He became my travel companion; loving me without condition. He was by my side guiding me on my path to gaining wisdom. But His attempts to guide me were a challenge. I was untamed and wanted to live a life using substances to distract me from my psychological pain. Jesus used these distractions to help me. Anytime I had a court date for breaking traffic laws, instead of tapping me on the shoulder to make sure I remembered, He let me forget. Jesus knew in my life filled with empty sex and too many drugs, that jail was my rehabilitation from that life. My forgotten court dates created arrest warrants that were my ticket to rehab. These warrants brought me to a place of quiet where I could eat properly, sober up, assess my life and read my Bible. A place where I could listen to God's messages of hope through the Christian ministry that existed inside the jails. This is why Jesus kept bringing me back to these places and why in the first few years of being in Colorado, I ended up visiting these jails regularly.

Jesus knew I had free will and He couldn't force me to stop my distractions. He wasn't going to step in and knock the joint or bubble pipe out of my hand. He wasn't going to make it so girls didn't like me. He let me pursue my path of self-destruction because it was only by reaching the bottom of my life that I would be able to rebuild the crumbling foundation of my childhood with a new one.

He let me continue to self-destruct because He knew the only way I'd want to change my life is when the pain got too bad that I'd welcome a change. He let me crash and burn because that's the only way He knew the change would be permanent.

Jesus showed me unconditional love throughout my early decades of adulthood, but I couldn't recognize it. To help me see His pure love working in my life He sent me a living, breathing example of His undemanding love. He gave me my son.

My son, Tanner was a physical example of Jesus' love. Right under my nose was what I longed for my whole life. Someone whose love was unconditional and unwavering when I couldn't love myself. Someone whose smile made me feel that regardless of who I was, it was enough to be loved by somebody.

Whenever I canceled weekends with Tanner because I was in jail for missing court dates, he still loved me. When my home was a discarded camper on the back of some pickup truck in a field, he still loved me. When my mind was in a fog because I was sneaking hits of meth during the weekends he visited me, he still loved me. When my primary residence was a mattress in the corner of an automobile garage, he still loved me. When I took him to a store to involve him in shoplifting merchandise, he still loved me. Regardless of the bad decisions or choices I made in my life, Jesus used Tanner to help me experience the true, undemanding love He had been showing me behind the scenes since I was fifteen.

Jesus and Tanner were the loving tag team that would save me from myself and play an important role in helping me keep my promise to turn my life around.

But first I had to deal with third-degree burns to my feet and legs.

26 STARTING OVER?

After the fire trucks left and the burnt remains of my life smoldered outside, I rested on Martell's couch thinking about what I'd lost and what I had done. In that camper were all my cherished possessions – my shoes, clothes, a valuable collection of sports memorabilia, my meth, and, unfortunately, even my son's pet rabbit.

How would I rebuild my life? Could I do it differently this time? Could I keep my promise to Jesus? The answers would have to wait. I had third-degree burns on my feet and legs and the meth I'd smoked before the fire was wearing off. I had rejected help from the paramedics when I was high, but soon I'd need to have my burns treated.

Martell could see my injuries and sensed my discomfort. Even though he had every right to be upset because the fire spread to his garage and damaged an antique car of his fathers, he showed me compassion and let me crash on his couch until the discomfort of my burns woke me and I called the Salvation Army for help. They came to his house and assessed my immediate needs. They gave me a used pair of shoes and an emergency kit with a blanket and a $350 Visa gift card.

By then the pain in my feet and legs was getting close to unbearable. I needed to get relief so I apologized to Martell for the damages and left. The meth was almost worn off and the numbing it provided was fading. The burning pain was intensifying. I called my dealer and used the Visa gift card to get more meth and a motel room.

My efforts to turn my life around were already heading in the wrong direction. I was in pain and as I always did, I turned to drugs. High on meth and getting little relief from the pain, I left the motel. Not thinking clearly, I planned to limp to Outlook Tavern to tell my bar buddies about the fire.

Even with the help of the meth, the discomfort and

difficulty walking continued. The burns were getting infected. They got so bad that shortly I was forced to seek out help at a rapid transit bus station along the way. I sat on the sidewalk in utter despair and flagged down a transit officer who called 911. Paramedics arrived and took me to the hospital.

I didn't have insurance but I knew the hospital couldn't refuse me treatment. They tended to my burns and bandaged my legs. I called Erika and she brought Tanner to see me. His smile uplifted my spirits and lessened the pain. In the early morning, I was released.

The morning I left the hospital was chilly and my burnt skin was particularly sensitive to the cool temperatures. I needed to get some pants and a coat. With my brain and pocket full of meth I slipped back into my old life. I walked into a Walmart to boldly shoplift some supplies. I limped into the store with bandaged legs I caught the attention of store security. Trying to leave the store with new pants and a jacket, they stopped me and called the police.

A female police officer responded to their call. She ran my name and found I had an outstanding arrest warrant. She also found the meth. I had enough to be charged with felony possession. Noticing my misery from the leg and feet burns, she made no mention of finding the meth in her report. I was still going to jail, but I'd only be facing months for a shoplifting charge rather than years for felony possession of drugs.

While my efforts to turn my life around weren't going so well, Jesus' plan to get me back into prison rehab was working perfectly. He had bigger plans for my recovery and they started with my jail time being longer but more productive than punishing.

27 PRISON REHAB

At Jefferson County jail I got the care I needed for my burns and a sober place to live. With access to quality medical attention, my burns slowly healed and my lack of meth cleared my head. Normally my times in jail were short. This stay was going to be much longer.

I went before a Jefferson County judge for my shoplifting charge and probation violation. I was sentenced to ninety days in jail. That much time away from drugs was three times what I would typically get had I gone into a regular rehab program. Jesus was doing His best to get me permanently sober.

During the start of my three-month stay in Jefferson

County, I was transferred to Adams County Sheriff's Detention Facility for the outstanding felony arrest warrant for another drug possession charge in that county.

In front of the judge for the felony charge, I told him about how I was determined to turn my life around and be a better influence in my little son's life. Jesus was with me that day because the judge reduced the felony charge to a misdemeanor and probation. I was released back to Jefferson County Jail. Whereas Jefferson County Jail was a well-run organization, professional and efficient, Adams County facility was a rag-tag, disorganized mess. The Adams County judge had signed off on my return to Jefferson County Jail, but then Adams County failed to process the transfer for a month!

I sat in Adams County Sheriff's Detention Facility for thirty days, forgotten by the people who needed to fill out the paperwork to release me back to Jefferson County Jail. Did Jesus have a hand in delaying my release? Looking back, I believe He did because while I sat in jail doing nothing I discovered an inspiring book called *The Shack*.

This book spoke to me deeply. The main character, Mack, lived with a childhood hurt because of an alcoholic father. The woman Mack married was named Nan, just like my grandmother. In the story, during a camping trip, Mack's daughter is abducted and brutally killed by someone. Mack went into a deep depression. Later in the story, Mack happened upon a shack in the middle of the woods where he met God in the form of an old black woman. They spent the weekend discussing love, hurt, and just punishment for the man who killed Mack's daughter. In the end, Mack realized the overwhelming compassion and understanding of God and how everyone, no matter how broken they are, can experience God's love and forgiveness. The book helped me realize that even with all my failings, there was a place in God's heart for me.

That book inspired me to take my words to the Adams County judge seriously. I decided with a clear and sober mind that I was done wasting my life and hurting those I loved through my selfish and irresponsible actions.

I recognized that I had become my father, an irresponsible, intoxicated joke. I had a growing son who needed a proper role model and my two nephews, Reece and Blake who looked to me to supplement the lessons of manhood they gained from Tyler. Young men were looking to me for an example and what they were getting up until now was disappointing at best.

I got on my knees next to the bed in my jail cell and prayed to Jesus. "Lord, you came into my life when I was young, yet I spent most of my adult life ignoring you. But even so, you came through for me when I needed your help to escape the fire. I'm going to keep my promise to you with your help. Guide my efforts to stay sober and change my life for the better. Whatever path you lead me on, I will accept it and follow you." I felt a warmth and calm wash over my body. I knew right then my efforts to keep my promises would be possible because I had Jesus beside me. Even with His help, I still had a rough road ahead.

28 NEW BEGINNINGS

Eventually, I was transferred back to Jefferson County Jail. I made a collect call to my mother and we talked about everything that happened to me. I told her about my promise to Jesus. She said she was coming to Colorado to see me.

I was excited about her visit and didn't want to be stuck in jail while she was in Colorado. I also missed my son. I petitioned to get my ninety-day sentence shortened because of the extended time I spent in the Adams County facility. I planned to ask that the remainder of my sentence be converted to probation. Moments before I saw the Jefferson County judge I prayed to Jesus. "Lord be with me. Guide my words.

Help me to find my way out of these jails and stay sober so I can be the type of father Tanner needs."

At the hearing were Jefferson County judge Joan Woodford and a probation officer who was all too familiar with my track record of ignoring the requirements of my previous probations. If this officer had her way, my ninety-day sentence would be extended indefinitely.

Judge Woodford asked why she should shorten my stay.

"Your honor," I started, "I'm ready to do things differently. I'm motivated to be a better man. The fire that burned my legs took away everything in my life, my home, and all my stuff. This is a great chance for me to start a new life and keep my promise to Jesus."

"JESUS?! Your Honor!" the probation officer shouted as she jumped out of her seat.

"Sit down, officer, you'll have your time to speak," demanded the judge. "Continue, Mr. Morse."

"Yes, Your Honor, when I was trapped in the burning camper where I lived I promised Jesus if He helped me escape, I would change my ways. And here I am. He saved me!" I continued. "I'm also motivated to change for my mother. She's always rooted for me and she's coming to town. I feel this time I can make her proud. I also have a six-year-old son whom I miss dearly and I've got two nephews who look up to me. I want to be a better dad for him and an uncle to them. Plus I finally want to be the sibling my brother deserves. I've alienated him with all my misbehaving. He's always given a lot to me and all I've done is take. I've got so many reasons to start doing things differently."

Judge Woodford then allowed my probation officer to speak.

"Your honor, Mr. Morse has shown a blatant disregard for the requirements of every probation he's had. He has never returned our calls and has missed every scheduled visit we've set. He has no respect for the judicial system or the probation process."

"Is this true, Mr. Morse? Have you ignored your probation responsibilities?" the judge asked.

"Yes, your honor. I've been struggling with drug

abuse and meth addiction and it has impacted every aspect of my life. But I've been sober for over a month now and I want to stay this way!"

The judge continued. "I've looked over your history of arrest warrants and it looks like you also disregard your responsibilities to appear in court for hearings. What I see is a pattern of contempt for our judicial system. Do either of you have anything to add?"

"No, your honor," my probation office responded.

"Your honor," I added, "now that I'm sober I want to stay this way. I'm going to rehab and have a plan in place for finding a facility."

She closed the thick file on her bench and deeply sighed. She leaned forward and addressed me. "Travis, I sense a genuine sincerity in your voice and believe that this time you are serious about improving for yourself, your mother, son, nephews, brother, and even Jesus. I'm going to rule to transfer the rest of your sentence to probation. But I warn you, Mr. Morse," she scolded, "if I hear from any officer that you've missed even one of your probation appointments or you violate probation, break any laws, regardless of how minor, I will have you back in Jefferson County jail serving out the rest of your sentence and with the addition of a contempt of court charge on top of it. You also have to get into a drug rehabilitation program immediately."

"Thank you, your honor. I made a promise to Jesus and I make a promise to you that I will change."

The parole officer packed up her paperwork and gave me a look signaling her disgust at how she believed I tricked the judge into releasing me.

After my release from Jefferson County Jail, I needed a place to stay until I found a rehab center. My only hope was at my brother Tyler's home, but at that point we were estranged because of my total disregard for anyone but myself while I pursued my meth habit.

"Jesus," I prayed before I called him, "Please soften my brother's heart. Let him show me forgiveness so I have a safe place to stay until I can find a rehab." Then I called him. Fortunately, he took my call. I told him about the fire and jail and my promise to Jesus. I told him I was checking myself into rehab as soon as I secured a place from one of the facilities on a list given to me by the Jefferson County Jail. I told him the safest place I could stay until then would be his place. He agreed to let me stay with him for a day or two until I entered a drug treatment program.

The next day I made some calls to rehab facilities, but each had a long waiting list. I had two facilities left to contact and thought if I visited them instead of calling, maybe I'd have better luck. I went downtown to one of the remaining rehab facilities, but being there in person didn't make a difference. After reviewing my situation they told me I didn't meet their qualifications for immediate admittance. Dejected I left their facility and sat at a picnic table in front of their building. Soon they came out and told me to get off of their property. I didn't know what to do.

I was at the end of the list of recommended rehab programs. There was one more place for me to try called New Beginnings Recovery Center. When I called I reached Mary Brewer. I told her about the miserable story of my life and how I needed to get into a rehab program. She empathized, then apologized that all the beds in her center were taken. She offered to add me to the tall stack of applications on her desk. Despondent, I sat on the phone speechless and silently prayed, "*Jesus help me.*" Then, instead of hanging up Mary blurted out the question, "How fast can you get here?!" Excitedly I told her where I was and the public transportation I'd need to take to reach her center. She said, "Well, get here as fast as you can!"

When I arrived at New Beginnings Recovery Center I understood why there was a waiting list. The center looked like a well-maintained medical clinic with a welcoming feel to it. It was much better than the jails I'd just left and certainly better than the other places drugs had taken me like the borrowed camper, automobile garage, storage sheds, and portable toilet.

As we talked, I told her about the many rejections I'd experienced while looking for rehab programs around the city. She agreed that the lack of beds at rehab facilities was a growing problem. Then I reminded her that she also initially rejected me and asked her why she changed her mind. She said, "I was ready to let you go find another program when Jesus spoke to me, telling me I needed to find a place for you in my program. I didn't know how I would do it, I just knew I needed to find a way. After we got off the phone I figured out that because you've been sober for a while now, I could allow you to stay at the Broadway House sober home across the street.

You can stay there and come over here to participate in the recovery programs during the day." She promised me thirty days at her center. I reminded her I had no possessions after the fire, including money, and she told me not to worry. She had scholarship money available to fund my stay.

Thank you, Jesus!

29 PROVING AND IMPROVING

The Broadway House sober home was a small ranch house within a few minutes walk of the rehab center. Sometimes up to six recovering addicts stayed there while they transitioned back into society. Staying at the sober home instead of the rehab center was a great blessing for me. I was already sober from going through prison rehab, and the handful of other people at the sober home were graduates of Mary's program and onto their next steps of staying sober.

Conversely, the people who stayed at the rehab

center were in the beginning stages of getting sober. They were a different crowd. It was not uncommon for these new clients to be high on something when they came to the rehab center on their first day. They knew they were going to be without their favorite drug once they entered rehab, so they got high "one more time" before giving it up for good. Like the smoker who chain smokes before quitting, or the person who binges on their favorite fattening foods before dieting, these addicts were reluctantly giving up something they loved and with that attitude, their chances of success were doomed.

There were a variety of reasons people with drug or alcohol addiction came to Mary's programs. Some were there because they were commanded by the courts to forced rehabilitation. Other addicts used rehab as a gesture to show family members or significant others that they were trying to get clean, but these were typically the ones who'd have their friends sneak them drugs during visitations. Still, others had every intention to get sober but didn't have enough resolve to leave what they loved behind. With unmotivated groups like this, the success rates for rehabilitation facilities were typically dismal. Of the dozen addicts who went through the program with me, after a year only two stayed sober. Of those who relapsed, four died of drug overdoses.

The failure rate certainly wasn't a reflection of Mary Brewer's dedication to the recovery programs. She cared deeply for each client in her rehab centers and designed her programs so those who wanted to succeed had the best chance of doing so.

Mary was an ordained Christian minister so Jesus was very much at the forefront of her recovery program. She delivered spiritual messages each week during Sunday services and we had daily Bible study. She didn't incorporate Jesus into the program to win followers to Christianity. She did it because faith-based programs have proven to significantly increase an addict's chances of success.

From the first day there, I felt at home at New Beginnings and very quickly stepped up my participation. I befriended Leo, the Bible study leader and he let me present an introduction to the Bible for beginners in the group.

When I first started reading the Bible back in my teens, I had no idea where to start reading. I somehow discovered that the book of Proverbs was a great place to start. That book has thirty-one verses;

one for each day of the month. During my presentation, I taught the group to look at the day of the month, then read and ponder that numbered verse from Proverbs. I also found Psalms to be encouraging and suggested they read them when looking for inspiration.

Besides doses of Christianity, Mary offered traditional programs as well. There were group meetings: Crystal Meth Anonymous, Alcoholics Anonymous, Cocaine Anonymous, and Narcotics Anonymous. Regardless of our addiction, we were required to attend all of these meetings to support each other. We had regular group therapy and one-on-one sessions. To teach us life skills like planning, cooperation, and responsibility, Mary gave us group projects and individual chores to do around the center. Mary also utilized scientific treatments such as Low Energy Neurofeedback which stimulates the brain to help reset it. It was a full schedule of supportive activities that were only as effective as the recovering addict's desire to gain from them.

I was determined to succeed and prove to my family I could do it. Most importantly, I wanted to be a clean and sober dad for Tanner, and keep my promise to Jesus and the judge. I kept my distance from the other addicts because I was all too familiar with their fake sincerity and self-serving antics. I came for a specific goal and with the help of Jesus, I was determined to achieve it.

The only person from the program I did befriend was a woman who welcomed me on the first day I entered the rehab center to start my recovery. I distinctly remember her big smile as she held open the door and said, "Hi, I'm Paige. Welcome to NBRC."

Paige was very pretty and friendly, but I emotionally kept my distance because I knew about the trap I could fall into if I tried to have anything more than a friendly relationship with her while trying to reprogram my mind to stay sober. We saw each other often in the various recovery programs and she seemed genuinely nice. I learned she came from a supportive Christian family, very much like the one my friend Joshua welcomed me into when I was fifteen.

Being committed to my recovery helped me make steady improvements. As the weeks went by, I took a leadership role in the Narcotics Anonymous group. Mary recognized my progress by graduating me a week early. She let me continue helping her clients at the rehab center, and I started working part-time at the local pizza place to ease my way back into society. I also used the pizza money to start paying rent to Mary.

Jesus led me to this blessed woman and her rehab program. I enjoyed my days there working on my recovery. My passion to heal made the activities feel effortless and living at the Broadway House provided me with a stress-free home. Until it wasn't.

30 SAVED LIVES

After six months of living at the sober house and helping at the rehab center, Mary made me a Client Liason. My duties were to screen new clients and their visitors who entered the recovery center. I'd check them and their belongings to ensure no drugs or alcohol were being snuck into the building. Mary also had me trained in some basic medical procedures because new members of the program regularly suffered withdrawal symptoms shortly after entering the center. I learned how to monitor people's vital signs. She also had me go through the Q.M.A.P. program which is Colorado's Qualified Medication Administration Personnel program for learning to properly dispense medications.

I asked Mary if I could be a sponsor for some of the newly sober clients at the Broadway House because they were coming to me for support. It's unconventional for a recovering addict to become a sponsor so soon in their sobriety journey. Being a sponsor meant I'd be helping recovering addicts stay on the straight and narrow path to recovery. Sponsors usually have to show a proven track record of sobriety so they can understand firsthand the challenges of long-term sobriety and act as an example of what's possible through prolonged sober living. Mary agreed to let me take on those responsibilities.

After a year of working at New Beginnings and living at the sober house, Mary hired me to manage the residents of Broadway House. She had witnessed my service to others and put me in charge of addicts who graduated to the sober living home. This was a challenge because some of the residents at the home were clever addicts who knew how to work the system to graduate. But they weren't mentally committed to being sober and I had to deal with many of their relapses.

The first was a young addict named Lucas. He was a heroin addict who managed to graduate into the sober home. Residents in the home had the freedom to come and go as long as they were back in the house by the 10 PM curfew. I had high hopes for Lucas and helped him get a job at the pizza place nearby. One Saturday night I saw him enter the home as he returned from work. As we talked I noticed his eyelids were drooping.

"Is something going on with you, Lucas?" I asked.

"Nothin'," he lied.

I let him go to his room, but I knew something wasn't right. A few minutes later I went to his bedroom to ask him again.

He was sitting on the edge of his bed just staring. "Lucas, are you on something?" He sat droopy-eyed and denied it. As I stood in front of him I watched Lucas's head bob as if he fought to stay conscious. It's a typical move of someone strung out on heroin referred to as "nodding out."

His head dropped to one side and he fell back onto his bed. I rushed over to check his vitals and he wasn't breathing. This was the first overdose I ever experienced and I ran to the cabinet to get Narcan (Naloxone Hydrochloride). We kept Narcan nasal spray for times like this. One shot of the spray usually revived someone who overdosed on opiates.

I brought back the Narcan, but was so nervous I accidentally squeezed it and it shot the life-saving mist into the air. Time was running out and I got another spray from the cabinet and squeezed it into his nose. But the Narcan spray did nothing. He still wasn't breathing!

I'd learned C.P.R. (cardiopulmonary resuscitation) but in the fog of trying to save Lucas, I couldn't remember the exact steps. I did remember something about breathing air into a person's lungs so I squeezed his nose and blew four big breaths into his lungs inflating his chest like a balloon. Lucas exhaled and regained consciousness. I called 911 and kept him awake until they arrived. He said, "Thanks, man," as if I'd just lent him five dollars rather than saved his life. In the coming days, he'd overdose again.

Lucas was just one of the sober home relapses.

Another resident, Mark, came back to the sober home one evening high on meth, and one Saturday night when I had my son visiting, another resident, Ethan, overdosed on heroin. His bedroom was across from mine in the basement. It was a makeshift bedroom that only had hanging sheets to separate his area from the rest of the basement. My son was in my bedroom playing video games while I went upstairs to do a night check of the residents. I was coming back down the stairs to go to my bedroom when I noticed an opening between the sheets and saw Ethan hunched over a table in his room. I rushed to check his vital signs. He had overdosed. I hurried to administer Narcan while my six-year-old son was feet away behind my closed bedroom door unaware of the drama playing out nearby. Fortunately, Ethan survived.

Whenever sober home residents relapsed Mary took them back to the rehab center. She gave the addicts in her programs unlimited chances to get it right. She was a tough woman with a no-nonsense attitude toward addiction or tolerance for drug abuse and she also had a kind and nurturing side to her personality. We affectionately called this tough woman "Mother Mary." I called her my lifesaver.

31 SELF-LOVE

In high school, I used popularity to distract me from the painful feelings of having no self-worth and I boosted my broken self-esteem by impressing others. Eventually, when popularity wasn't enough, I supplemented my efforts to quiet the pain and enhance my feelings of euphoria with weed, alcohol, and narcotics.

A lot had changed since those high school days. Once I became a fixture at New Beginnings, I gained a reputation as a valued member of their staff and I built a new type of self-esteem based on how well I provided service to others. My desire to serve my fellow man replaced my need to impress people.

At New Beginnings my self-worth was fed by my Bible students who found a new value in that old book. It was uplifted when I stopped visitors from bringing in illegal substances that endangered our clients' efforts for successful rehabilitation. My self-worth grew with each addict who called on me as a sponsor to help them through rough patches as they tried to maintain sobriety. It was boosted when I brought overdosed addicts back to life so they could give their rehabilitation another chance.

As my self-worth grew, so did my self-love and its positive influence eased the pain of my childhood trauma. By living in service to others I now had complete control of who I was and how I felt about myself. For the first time in my life, I liked who I was. No longer was I affected by someone else's opinion of me. No longer did I have negative self-esteem that sabotaged my efforts to be a better person.

With this improved self-esteem came the confidence that a life of sobriety was very possible and with

Jesus' help maintaining sobriety looked downright easy. Of course it looked easy; I was living in the sheltered world of New Beginnings with no temptations or stress. My daily schedule kept my mind occupied with sobriety activities, and helping others offered its own kind of high.

But New Beginnings wasn't the real world. I was sober in a place where none of my friends were offering to share drugs with me. Living in the sober home I was isolated from pressures such as making mortgage payments, fears of losing my job, car problems, arguments with a spouse, nursing sick kids, or any of the other day-to-day challenges that test our resolve to handle life's problems soberly. New Beginnings was a utopia for sobriety.

What would happen once I entered real life and something shook my confidence and triggered pain that threatened my sobriety? Would I still be able to face it without drugs and trust Jesus to guide me through it? I was about to find out.

32 THE TEST

Trusting God is an ongoing theme in the Bible. Over and over we read stories of how God asked people to trust Him so they could enjoy the best life. In the Old Testament, we read these kinds of stories about Adam, Noah, Moses, Joshua, Caleb, Isaiah, and my favorite story of trusting God - the story of Abraham and Sarah.

God promised childless Abraham that he would have a son to carry on his lineage. Such a promise would be a miracle because his wife Sarah was not able to have children. But instead of Abraham trusting that

God would make good on His promise, he and Sarah reasoned that maybe God meant Abraham was supposed to have a son with the help of another woman. They came up with a plan to have Abraham sleep with Hagar, a handmaid. She got pregnant and they had a son, Ishmael. But that wasn't God's plan, it was theirs. God again promised Abraham that he would have a son and told him his wife Sarah would be a mother of nations. Abraham laughed in disbelief. He knew it was impossible. Abraham was one hundred years old and his wife was ninety. But then the impossible happened. Sarah got pregnant by Abraham and Isaac was born. Isaac meant everything to Abraham because he was the miracle baby who held the promise of giving Abraham descendants.

God knew how much Abraham loved his new son, but God wanted to teach Abraham to be confident that trusting Him was always the best approach when facing challenges. God created a test to help Abraham see that.

When Isaac became a young man, God commanded Abraham to take his son Isaac up to a mountain and sacrifice his son's life. As illogical as this command seemed, Abraham remembered that God's previous illogical promise come true and trusted God without question. When Abraham reached the mountaintop and was ready to take his precious son's life with a knife, an angel stopped him. Abraham had proven to God, and himself, that he truly trusted God's plans even if those plans seemed illogical and might have cost him his beloved son.

My test for how much I trusted God started with a frantic phone call from Erika one evening telling me she was at the hospital emergency room with Tanner. Erika was doing remodeling at her home and had a disposal company put a large rectangular metal dumpster in her driveway for collecting the construction debris. Erika said she warned Tanner to stay away from that dumpster, but he was curious and swung open the large metal door at the end of it to step inside. As he entered the dumpster, the large door swung back toward him and crushed his thin body between the door and a corner of the side wall. Tanner was critically injured and managed to make his way back into the house to tell his mother what had happened. She rushed him to the local hospital.

When I met them at the hospital, the emergency doctors had done some preliminary tests and scans and determined they were not qualified to treat his injuries. He needed to be airlifted to Children's

Hospital, one of the best in the country. His prognosis was not good.

I called everyone I knew, Tyler, my mother, Paige, Mary Brewer, and her son Chris who had become my close friend. They all said they'd meet me at the hospital.

At Children's, a team of specialists discovered Tanner was bleeding internally from his portal vein. It's the main vein that drains the blood from the gastrointestinal tract, gallbladder, pancreas, and spleen to the liver. To access the vein and stop the bleeding they would have to slice open his torso, pull the organs out of his abdomen, and hope the damage they found was reparable.

By the time I arrived, they were rolling him into surgery. I looked at Tanner and tried to show a positive smile as I kissed him and told him I loved him. I realized my only reason for living was lying on that hospital gurney stuck with needles, hooked up to bags of fluid, and connected with sensors in hopes of prolonging his life. At that moment nothing mattered to me but his survival. My precious son was bleeding to death and I couldn't save him.

For the next eight hours as Erika and I sat in the

waiting room, our group of supporters grew. Erika's family arrived, Paige came, and my brother Tyler brought some of our friends. My mother and Chris Brewer were on flights heading to be with me.

While we waited, our group prayed a lot and handed over the situation to Jesus. I was sober so I had no more bargaining chips to offer Jesus. In total anguish, I humbly asked Him to grant me a miracle to save my precious son. At that moment I imagined the pang God must have felt when He watched Jesus dying on the cross. Despite the dismal outlook, I believed Jesus still offered me hope.

After surgery, Tanner was brought back to the Intensive Care Unit. I'll never forget seeing him. He was lying there with tubes and tape and sensors and fluid bags. The skin on his torso was dyed orange from the iodine painted on him before surgery. His abdomen had been sliced open and his organs were exposed so doctors could visually monitor the repair behind them.

When the surgeon came in to discuss his injuries with Erika and me, my mind was in a fog. The doctor used a lot of medical jargon but all I wanted to hear was that Jesus delivered a miracle and Tanner was out of danger. Instead, my heart sank as the doctor talked about the damage to his insides that required the removal of one of his kidneys, his spleen, and part of his pancreas. The conversation ended with him giving Tanner a ten percent chance of survival.

33 TWENTY-ONE DAYS

When I was trapped in the camper fire, I saw firsthand how Jesus turned around a desperate and deadly situation. Burned into my memory, that experience would forever feed my belief Jesus could do anything.

While our group prayed in the waiting room, Erika and I sat silently by Tanner's bedside listening to the rhythmic clicking and beeping of the monitors. I bowed my head and said a silent prayer to Jesus. "*Lord, I know nothing is impossible for you. I've seen how you've worked miracles in my life and others. Please be with my son in his hour of need and if it is the will of The Father that he should live, please help guide him through this so that he and others will see your glory and praise God.*"

Ending my prayer I sat there in silence. Then I heard a reassuring whisper break through the beeps and clicks that said, "He will survive." Jesus had heard my prayer. But then I wondered. *Is that all he will do… survive? Will this accident leave him physically crippled for the rest of his life?*

I didn't tell anyone about the whisper in my head and encouraged everyone to continue to pray for him.

For the next twenty-one days, Erika and I stayed with Tanner. The hospital provided places for us to sleep so we could stay there day and night. Mary generously paid my wages the entire time and organized a donation drive to help us with expenses.

Every day was touch and go. His week in the Intensive Care Unit was the most critical and when they put him in a regular hospital room after a week, the doctors still questioned his long-term survival. Thanks to Jesus' reassurance I knew better.

Over those three weeks, my group and I continued

to pray. Clients at New Beginnings formed a prayer circle to help. Every prayer helped heal his body. On the day we finally left the hospital with Tanner, I looked to the sky and thanked Jesus for once again showing me His ability to accomplish feats against impossible odds.

Tanner made a complete recovery and became a healthy, happy young man who likes biking and is proficient at karate. I thank Jesus every day for the gift of having my son in my life and for providing me with a resource to depend on when life presents challenges that could endanger my sobriety. Once I'd passed the test and learned nothing could undermine my faith in Jesus, it was time to learn another lesson - forgiveness.

34 THE CALL

For most of my life, I've carried around the wounded self-image that I was unlovable because my father abandoned me. As my life turned around and I made it to the other side of my addiction, I was able to take a sober look back and have empathy for the hurting child I was back then. With my newfound self-love, I was able to see that hurt drove my actions and I gained a new understanding and compassion for my inner child who was hurt and looking for love.

In the 12th chapter of Mark, Verse 31, Jesus says the second greatest commandment for man is to love others *as we love ourselves.* Before I could offer genuine love to others I had to gain a love for myself. Once I finally loved myself, I had love to share, and did that through service to the addicts at New Beginnings. Now I needed to take sharing my love to the next level. I needed to show love, understanding, and compassion to those who hurt me.

The opportunity came when I got a call from my mother one evening. She told me my father wanted to talk to me. I didn't understand why this man, who'd hurt me with his desertion and was never a part of my life, wanted to talk. But in keeping with my new spirit of compassion and understanding, I told my mom I'd agreed to speak to him.

In recovery, I learned that my father's actions were not a reflection of who I was, but who he was. Healthy people don't hurt people, hurting people hurt others. I healed my self-image by separating my self-worth from his act of abandonment and rebuilt it by sharing love through service to others. My self-image was based on the loving person I'd become and not someone who was the victim of others' actions or opinions.

My mom said my father was going to call me after dinner on Friday. I was reluctant to take his call but my mom encouraged me to speak to him. To prepare myself mentally, I turned to the Bible. I found this verse 11 in Chapter 19 of Proverbs:

> *"A person's wisdom yields patience; it is to one's glory to overlook an offense."*

Further in Proverbs, I found in the 25th chapter, Verse 21:

> *"If your enemy is hungry, give him food to eat; if he is thirsty, give him water to drink."*

The Bible was telling me to extend compassion to someone who may not have shown it to me.

I continued randomly searching the Bible and Jesus led me to the New Testament where I found the message of forgiveness repeated there as well. When Jesus taught people the Lord's Prayer He said to ask God to, "Forgive us our trespasses *as we forgive the trespasses of others.*" In the Beatitudes, Matthew writes in Chapter 5, Verse 7 that Jesus praised people who showed mercy. And when Peter asked Jesus if seven times is enough to forgive others who hurt us, Jesus replied in Matthew Chapter 18, Verse 22 "…not seven times, but seventy times seven."

It was clear Jesus was leading me to Bible passages

showing that forgiving my father was the next step on my spiritual journey.

When I answered my father's call I tried not to sound abrupt. "Hello?"

"Travis," came a weak voice in reply, "thanks for letting me talk to you…"

I could hear how a lifetime of drinking had taken its toll on this man. His words were slow and slurred.

"I know I screwed up, "he admitted, "I'm not doing well. I have to have my leg amputated…"

As I listened, a storm brewed in my head between the hurt child deep inside me and the loving man I had become. My traumatized inner child reasoned that my father needed to be hurt to pay for the hurt he caused others. A new part of me wanted to extend compassion to this fellow human to show I understood his pain. I certainly understood his addiction because we both followed similar paths of substance abuse and self-destruction. The difference was he was losing his battle and I had found a way to win mine. As the struggle raged on in my head, I simply acknowledged his comments, "Okay…"

"I'm sorry for leaving you guys… I'm sorry for all of that."

I learned an important lesson from my father abandoning us, especially when I had my son. I learned that the most important job a father has is to *be there* for his children. Be present in their lives. When I was young and my father disappeared, I took it personally and used immature logic to believe the problem was me. Had he been around showing me he wanted to be in my life, things would have been different. That's why after Tanner was born, I made a point to see my son often and let him know he was always in my heart. If I was heading to jail, I used my one phone call to let Tanner know he wouldn't hear from me because I was going away for a while. Regardless of how dismal my living arrangements were, I always asked Erika to let me have him on my weekends. Even when I was strung out on meth I made a point to attend his family and school functions. Being there for him was a job I took very seriously.

"I'm sorry," my father continued, "I don't have much time left. I'm not getting my leg amputated… I'm done with this life. I just called to ask you to forgive me."

"*Jesus, help me with my struggle. Help me do what's right,*" I silently prayed. I needed to learn to forgive my father's trespasses just as I'd learned to forgive my own. If I didn't forgive others, how could I expect to be forgiven?

I took a deep breath and lied to my father, "I forgive you."

Forgiving someone is hard. It doesn't mean forgetting the trauma we've experienced. It means not remembering the trauma with anger. I had a lot of anger to let go of. The thing about anger is it only hurts us. It's been said that holding on to anger is like grasping a hot coal with the intent of throwing it at someone else, but we are the only one who gets burned.

Getting rid of my anger wasn't going to happen cold turkey. Like sobriety, I had to work on it and with Jesus' help, I'd slowly achieve it one day at a time. Forgiving my father was the first step to helping me mend the hurt that happened so many decades earlier.
My father died a few days after the call.

With Jesus' help and guidance, my life had come full

circle. He's helped me work on closing the hurtful chapter that began my life, close the self-destructive chapters that made up my life before recovery and begin a new chapter by extending love to someone who hurt me deeply. Thanks to Jesus, that seemingly impossible transformation was being made possible.

I asked for strength…

and God gave me difficulties to make me strong.
I asked for wisdom…

and God gave me problems to learn to solve.
I asked for prosperity…

and God gave me a brain and brawn to work.
I asked for courage…

and God gave me dangers to overcome.
I asked for love…

and God gave me people to help.
I asked for favours…

and God gave me opportunities.
I received nothing I wanted.
I received everything I needed.

Hazrat Inayat Khan

35 EPILOGUE

As of this writing, I have been sober for over five years. I'm enjoying living my faith with Paige and her family. Tanner is closer to me than ever and I take him on frequent fishing and camping trips in the mountains of Colorado. I'm finally the sibling my brother Tyler deserves and the kind of uncle to Reece and Blake I hoped to be.

Over the past five years, I've given my testimony in front of fellow addicts at recovery centers and have been encouraged to share my stories with even more people. That's why I wrote this book.

If you have a group that you think would benefit from the stories and messages in this book, please contact me at AuthorTravisMorse@gmail.com to discuss a speaking engagement or quantity purchases of this book.

Made in the USA
Columbia, SC
29 May 2023

9b5f70ff-9f2f-4590-8311-ecccd0958e5bR01